Bad Grades Happen to Good Teachers

Creating Environments Where All Students LEARN

Linda Bress Silbert, Ph.D.
Alvin J. Silbert, Ed.D.

A **STRONG** LEARNING CENTERS® Publication

Why Bad Grades Happen to Good Teachers

Creating Environments Where
All Students LEARN

by Linda Bress Silbert, Ph.D. and Alvin J. Silbert, Ed.D.

Published by Strong Learning Publications

Copyright © 2014 Linda Bress Silbert & Alvin J. Silbert

ISBN: 978-0-89544-218-5

10 9 8 7 6 5 4 3 2 1

To our teachers
for pointing us in the right direction;
to all teachers who continue to
blaze new trails in that direction.

Also by the same authors

Why Bad Grades Happen to Good Kids
(2007, Beaufort Books, NY)

Strong Learning Centers® Books and Workbooks
Study Skills Workbooks (5 Titles - Grades 6-12)
Creative Thinking Workbooks (7 Titles - Grades K-6)
Beginning Reading Storybooks (8 Titles - Grades 1-4)
Make My Own Book Kits (7 Titles - Grades PreK-1)
Life Skills Program (6 Titles - Grades K-5)
Phonics Card Games (20 Titles - Grades K-6)
Strong Learning Center® Learning Games
Tiger Tuesday™ Learning Games

For more information, please visit:

www.StrongLearning.com
or
www.StrongLearningTeacherStore.com

CONTENTS

Contents

Introduction

Keeping Our Eyes on the Mission

It's crazy these days.

Administrators fear loss of funding based on the test scores of their students. Teachers fear that they will be held accountable for results on new testing methods they have not had time to review — much less create lesson plans that align with them — and that their evaluations will be negatively affected. Business leaders fear that we will lose our competitive edge in the world.

In our tutoring practice, we see the "fallout" almost daily, where we cannot afford to see it — *in the children themselves:*

- Eight-year-olds with too much homework — punished for not finishing it and required to write "I am ashamed of myself";
- Seventh graders who can spout off multiple-choice answers with no understanding of what the words or concepts mean;
- Children who are struggling in school labeled or grouped without regard for the labels' impact on their self-confidence;

- Kids of all ages terrified of standardized tests because they've been told by parents or teachers that they'll be held back if they don't do well. (And, as a result of their anxiety, they don't.)

We live in an electronic world where information is at our fingertips 24/7 and in a more globally-oriented society that will require that our children compete in an economic reality much different from that we knew as kids. Because of new technologies, our students come to us with skills only a few of us could have imagined. A two-year-old can learn the alphabet by brushing her finger across a hand-held device.

However, although the skills and knowledge students need to learn seem to change every day and new learning standards and tests are adopted almost as quickly, human beings and the ways we learn have not changed. As a result, the mission of educators is the same today as it was years ago when we were in school—*to create an environment in which all students have the greatest opportunity to learn.*

In the decades we have worked with parents, teachers and administrators to help students improve their academic performance, we have seen time and again that facilitating achievement is simple in theory but not so simple to put into practice. We've used our 37 years in the classroom—eight in administration—and decades in our private tutoring practice to visit and re-visit all the strategies.

We've assembled the best—and easiest to carry out—strategies on how to create an environment that supports our universal mission. We call it the STRONG Learning model.

We've found that in every classroom, three global factors influence the success or failure of learning for each student:

the teacher, the student, and the health of the relationship between them. In this book, we devote a whole section to each factor— addressing what we have found through the years to be the most important issues unique with respect to each.

We know that the pressure is high. We know that as classroom sizes, student-teacher ratios and administrative reporting responsibilities have increased, the amount of time you've had available for your students has been squeezed.

But our mission is still the same.

There's no doubt. The explosion of new information we are called on to teach is overwhelming. The volume of new technologies available to our students expands daily. That's not going to change.

But if we as teachers, parents, administrators and other school personnel stay current with respect to new content and methods and keep our eyes on the mission— to create environments where all students have opportunity to learn and experience academic success— student test scores, school ratings, and teacher evaluations will all take care of themselves.

When we were in college, one of our professors began every class with a simple phrase, borrowed from an ad slogan popular at the time. "It's what's up front that counts."

She was right. There's no better place to start.

Please Note:

This book is a guide for teachers and other educators of children. It is not intended to be the basis of solving serious student or school problems. As noted throughout this book, in dealing with any crisis or serious situation, we urge you to discuss issues about students with appropriate colleagues at your school and then initiate a conference call or meeting with their parents to advise them about these issues or challenges.

Also note that throughout the text, numerous case studies have been included for illustrative purposes. They are actual case studies, but student identities have been fictionalized or disguised and names or other identifying characteristics have been changed.

PART I

The Teacher

Chapter I

Making the Grade as Teachers

The word "grades" in the title of this book refers to:

- Student "grades," both on in-class exams and standardized testing, assessments of what they've learned with respect to grade level concepts and subjects as now codified by the Common Core State Standards
- Teacher "grades" or ratings of effectiveness and skill. With respect to current standards for teacher evaluation, our model most aligns with the InTASC Standards as they are translated in the Danielson Framework.

In this book, we focus primarily on teacher "grades," as they profoundly, though indirectly, affect student grades.

Why do bad grades happen to good teachers? As you might have guessed from the introduction, we believe it's because those teachers *lose sight of the mission.*

In today's environment for teachers, that's easy to do. With educators' jobs and salaries increasingly dependent on student scores on standardized tests, the stakeholders who are likely to be affected most by "high stakes" testing are teachers. There's no question that, in the current economy, this real or perceived threat to one's livelihood is hard to ignore.

There's no question, either, that if your performance evaluation as a teacher is tied to outcomes over which you have no control, the practice is irrational. And to make matters worse, if your evaluation is utilized in a formula to determine what funding your district will receive, the travesty is compounded. If these things are true, then teachers are in the unenviable position of being required to play a game for which no one has bothered to supply the rules.

We think you'll agree that learning and performance standards like the Common Core and InTASC must continue to evolve as educators strive to keep up with the demands of an ever-changing workplace. Without learning standards, we have no way to assess our students' progress toward mastery of the skills and concepts they need to thrive. Without them, lesson planning and homework assignments are blind exercises.

For the same reasons, we need standards for evaluating teaching proficiency too. Teaching, after all, isn't a static profession — we too must strive for continuous improvement in our knowledge and skills.

To restore our focus on the mission of education, our first step must be, despite the current chaos, to determine what we can and cannot control. For instance, we cannot control what the legislatures do, what our school boards do or what our administrators do. We can only attempt to stimulate positive change by supporting those who work as advocates of our profession.

But we *can* control what we as individual teachers know about learning by staying "on top" of the latest developments. We *can* control what we do and say in our classrooms. And we *are* in charge of how prepared we are to address the unique issues that present themselves with the specific group of students with which we are working.

In simplest terms, teachers need to help their students acquire knowledge and skills they'll need to measure up on standardized exams. In order for this to happen, teachers need to create, adapt and maintain the environment—physically, emotionally and intellectually—in which students have the greatest opportunities to succeed in learning.

That's what this book is about—focusing on the things we as educators *can* control. We're convinced that if we keep our eyes on the goal of doing everything *in our power* to ensure that our students learn, neither the Common Core nor the InTASC standards will give any of us a problem.

In a recent "TED Talk" on education presented on PBS, Sir Ken Robinson related a story of California's Death Valley. He described a year in which seven inches of rain fell in a desert where the average annual rainfall is less than two inches. The following spring, the floor of the desert transformed itself into a meadow, covered with grasses and wildflowers. "What we learned," he said, "was that Death Valley isn't dead. It's *dormant.*"

Similarly, many of our students are dormant, ready to bloom when conditions are right. They are each unique—diverse in how they learn and the challenges they face. They are not "empty heads" into which we pour multiple-choice answers to be regurgitated on standardized tests.

At the same time, because our students are all young human beings, their basic needs are *not* diverse. In that, Abraham Maslow was right.

Second only to their parents, teachers have the greatest influence over students. Because of our stature in their lives, we have the power to boost or demolish their self-esteem, which, when realistically grounded, is the single-most important factor in engaging and sustaining achievement motivation, especially in the early years. Once positive self-esteem is established in children, maintaining it requires they develop an increasing sense of control over their lives and confidence in their ability to set goals and develop coherent plans to achieve them, which, in turn, fuels their taking ownership of maximizing their academic potential.

As you read, think about events in your own life—the teachers who inspired you, the teachers who scarred you. Emulate the teacher(s) in whose classrooms you discovered you could do things you were sure you couldn't. Examine your interactions with your students and purge them of any that, as a student, left *you* feeling diminished.

Like diverse plants in the same garden, if the climate is right and the soil is fertile, all students, irrespective of learning styles or disabilities, will put down roots, absorb the nutrients they need to grow, and learn what they need to succeed in the global workplace of the future, just as we learned what *we* needed to succeed.

Chapter 2

Are You a Professional Teacher or a Practitioner?

I was attending a parent-teacher conference with the recently-divorced parents of a child I was working with who was struggling in history. I talked about the results of my assessment — the fact that she had an expressive language disorder, its impact on her understanding of the way in which the teacher was delivering the material, and the emotional impact her parents' divorce had recently had in the child's life.

When I finished, the history teacher leaned back in his chair and said, "So, what's the point? I'm not a psychiatrist. I'm a history teacher. It's my job to teach history."

I was relating this to a friend and colleague who is a guidance counselor in the same school. She shook her head sadly. "Some teachers are professionals," she said. "And others are practitioners. There's a difference."

Subsequently, through our joint efforts, we were able to move the child into a history class taught by a professional and soon she was back on track to learn.

Think for a moment about why you became a teacher. Was it because:

A. You wanted a seasonal job, with summers off?
B. Education seemed like an easy major?
C. Job security was important to you?
D. You fully understood that what our students learn (or don't) will impact how they contribute to the health of our society and the role our nation plays in the world?
E. All of the above?

We hope you answered "E." Having said that, of course, if you became a teacher because of A) summers off, B) your perception that, as a major, education would be easier than say, architectural engineering, or C) because job security was important to you, we don't mean to imply there's anything wrong with that. These are traditionally the "perks" of being a teacher. But the perks of one's profession aren't what *define* it as a profession. So, what does?

The difference between a "practitioner" and a "professional" in education is not unlike the difference between a bookkeeper and accountant, a mechanic and an engineer, or a paralegal and a lawyer. Understanding more than a set of basic procedures, professionals know "the larger point" of what they're doing and their contribution in achieving it.

Our collective responsibility as teachers is huge. It extends, and always has, far beyond the hours of 8:00 to 3:00 for 10 months of a given year. Because we are the second line of defense in the lives of the children and youth we work with every day, what we do has a ripple effect.

That ripple will be positive or negative with respect to the future of our society and its prosperity.

By necessity, as with any paid position of responsibility irrespective of industry, jobholders must be evaluated periodically to ensure that they continue to have the knowledge and skills they must to achieve the outcomes expected from the job.

As Answer "D" addresses, we cannot afford to be practitioners because the stakes are too high. We must be able to distinguish between the practitioners and the professionals, and provide constructive feedback to those teachers committed to being and becoming professionals. There must be standards in place that allow teachers and teacher evaluators to be on the same page when discussing a given teacher's areas of proficiency and those job functions where they need to improve. That's what the InTASC standards represent.

Following is a summary of the InTASC standards, taken directly from the website of the Council of Chief State School Officers (*www.ccsso.org*).

The InTASC Standards

- **Standard #1: Learner Development.** The teacher understands how learners grow and develop, recognizing that patterns of learning and development vary individually within and across the cognitive, linguistic, social, emotional, and physical areas, and designs and implements developmentally appropriate and challenging learning experiences.

- **Standard #2: Learning Differences.** The teacher uses understanding of individual differences and diverse cultures and communities to ensure inclusive learning environments that enable each learner to meet high standards.

- **Standard #3: Learning Environments.** The teacher works with others to create environments that support individual and collaborative learning, and that encourage positive social interaction, active engagement in learning, and self-motivation.

- **Standard #4: Content Knowledge.** The teacher understands the central concepts, tools of inquiry, and structures of the discipline(s) he or she teaches and creates learning experiences that make the discipline accessible and meaningful for learners to assure mastery of the content.

- **Standard #5: Application of Content.** The teacher understands how to connect concepts and use differing perspectives to engage learners in critical thinking, creativity, and collaborative problem solving related to authentic local and global issues.

- **Standard #6: Assessment.** The teacher understands and uses multiple methods of assessment to engage learners in their own growth, to monitor learner progress, and to guide the teacher's and learner's decision making.

- **Standard #7: Planning for Instruction.** The teacher plans instruction that supports every student in meeting rigorous learning goals by drawing upon knowledge of content areas, curriculum, cross-disciplinary skills, and pedagogy, as well as knowledge of learners and the community context.

- **Standard #8: Instructional Strategies.** The teacher understands and uses a variety of instructional strategies to encourage learners to develop deep understanding of content areas and their connections, and to build skills to apply knowledge in meaningful ways.

- **Standard #9: Professional Learning and Ethical Practice.** The teacher engages in ongoing professional learning and uses evidence to continually evaluate his/her practice, particularly the effects of his/her choices and actions on others (learners, families, other professionals, and the community), and adapts practice to meet the needs of each learner.

- **Standard #10: Leadership and Collaboration.** The teacher seeks appropriate leadership roles and opportunities to take responsibility for student learning, to collaborate with learners, families, colleagues, other school professionals, and community members to ensure learner growth, and to advance the profession.

Several researchers have broken these general standards into more practical and measureable frameworks. One of the most popular, in use in New York and 14 other states as of this writing, is the Danielson Framework or "Placemat," which reorganizes the standards into four areas: Planning and Preparation, Classroom Environment, Instruction and Professional Responsibilities.

The professional teacher who closely reviews the InTASC standards or Danielson Framework will find little that he or she doesn't already know. I've asked teachers what they think about all the new standards. A common response is, "I'm not worried about the Common Core or InTASC. Good teachers have been doing this for years."

Despite this, the timing of the releases of the Common Core and InTASC standards (2010 and 2011) have made for a lot of confusion and a lot of misinformation, which, in turn, has stimulated unnecessary alarm for teachers, because of fears about their jobs.

We've looked at them closely and agree with those teachers. There is nothing in either of the "new" standards to fear. Here's why.

The idea behind the Common Core State Standards was to answer a single question: *What do our students need to know to succeed today and in the world of the future?* The name tells the rest—the intent was to define a "common core" group of concepts and skills that would be used across the country, hopefully in every state, so that students from Georgia, for example, would be learning the same things that students in California were learning.

So, a group of businesspeople, governors and some of our educational peers met and over a number of years, put together lists of the knowledge, skills and experiences American students must know at each age and grade level to be prepared to function—and function well—in the workplace today. That's it. The Common Core standards are meant for teachers to use to set objectives for their lesson plans.

The InTASC standards seek to answer another single question: *Are we, as teachers today, learning and doing everything we can to ensure that our students will learn what they need to know?*

For teaching professionals, that question, which forms the basis for our evaluations, isn't anything new. Professional teachers have only one goal: *to do everything in our power to ensure that our students learn what they need to know to succeed:*

- Staying on top of advancements in the subject matter, concepts and skills we have been employed to teach,
- Keeping up with and applying new methods suggested by ongoing research about how humans learn,

- Understanding and correctly identifying in individual students which of a variety of obstacles—intellectual, physical, emotional—may be interfering with their learning, and
- Persisting in working together with other teachers, school psychologists and guidance counselors, to find the best methods for overcoming those obstacles within the classroom.

In the end, the only goal of teaching is *student learning*. If students aren't learning, and bad grades are happening, either to them or to us, it is our job to determine what's going on and do whatever we can to either remove or go around what stands in their way...or *ours*.

Sometimes we will find that the reasons lie with the students. Are their brains ready for processing the level of information we're giving? Are our lesson plans geared for kids of all learning styles? Is something in their brains disrupting the "normal" pathway of learning?

Sometimes the reasons will lie with some part of the environment—the home climate from which they come and/or the classroom environment *you* create. Is a student hungry, tired, stressed, or depressed? Is your classroom a place where students are emotionally and physically safe? Is it a place where successes, no matter how small, are celebrated?

And sometimes the reasons will lie with *us*.

Are you doing everything you can to ensure that your students learn? Our hope for this book is to help you answer that question with a resounding, "Yes."

PART II

The Environment

Chapter 3

What Makes an Environment Conducive to Learning?

An environment conducive to learning is:

A. Physically safe and comfortable.
B. Emotionally safe and self-esteem enhancing.
C. Intellectually engaging, providing knowledge, skill, and a foundation for continued learning
D. One where the teacher is constantly aware of whether learning is taking place and adapting
E. All of the above.

Clearly, "E" is the answer here, but "A," which refers to a physically safe and comfortable environment is necessarily outside of the scope of this book. You know the size and shape of your room, the number of windows, the arrangement of tables and/or desks...and we don't.

But the first priority with respect to the physical organization of your classroom is the same as for all facets of the environment—to facilitate student learning. All components of the environment are at play—the physical arrangement of the classroom, the resources we employ (or don't), the methods we use to impart knowledge, the accuracy with which we assess and the professionalism with which we report student progress (especially to the students themselves), the ways we interact with our students on a day-to-day, hour-to-hour basis…all of them either increase the likelihood of learning or stand in its way.

Part II focuses primarily on answers B, C and D of the multiple-choice question, addressing the core intellectual and emotional elements of an environment conducive to learning — within the framework of what we've come to call the STRONG Model.

Chapter 4
The STRONG Model

"Try hard and you will succeed."
— Michael, Age 10 —

"You know, if I try hard and keep working at something, I will succeed."

That's what Michael, a square-shouldered fifth grader, told me as he sat down one day to read with me. "You're right, Michael," I answered quickly. I was thrilled to hear a child say that, especially Michael. He had severe language issues and we were working hard to help him compensate. When I say "we," I mean his mom, dad, grandparents, teachers and other professionals in and outside of school. He had a wonderful support system that accepted and respected him unconditionally.

"Who told you that?" I asked. "Your mom or dad?"
"No," answered Michael.

"One of your grandmas or grandpas?"

"No," answered Michael. "We went to the Chinese restaurant last night and it was in my fortune cookie, so it must be true."

Though I confess I don't have such faith in the "truth" of fortune cookies, one thing was certainly true for Michael. Whatever he did, whenever and wherever he did it, his entire family was there to cheer him on. This, no doubt, contributed significantly to his high self-esteem.

I first met Michael and his family when he was five years old. At that time, when he talked, no one could understand him.

Understandably, his family was concerned about how he would function in school and they were worried about his future. As a five-year-old, he had already spent three years working with neurologists, audiologists, pediatricians and speech therapists. He was diagnosed with aphasia, a language disorder that often made it difficult for him to speak and understand others. In Michael's case, he could not retrieve words or sounds, which made it difficult to understand anything he was saying as well. He also had dyslexia — a reading disorder — and wasn't able to connect sounds with their visual symbols.

My work with Michael continued through his elementary school years. Between his school support, which included hours of therapy with a well-qualified speech therapist, private tutoring sessions and assistance at home, Michael succeeded.

Were there rough times? Yes. Michael would often become so frustrated when he could not retrieve words that he would pound his fists on the table. But through it all, Michael's family never turned their backs on him. They accepted his strengths and weaknesses, supported him daily and respected his needs.

Why is Michael's story important? Because it shows that all students, even when the odds are against them from the get-go, can succeed in school and beyond.

However, *success doesn't just happen.* It results from the combined efforts of the child, his parents and his teachers to create the conditions in which success can happen. In Michael's case, because of his disabilities, it took a great deal of effort on all three fronts. But it happened — at the time of this writing, Michael is in college majoring in engineering. He is an amazing math student — and now he talks up a storm!

Why Do Kids Struggle in School?

School success may still be hard to attain for any student, whether or are not learning disabilities are present as they were with Michael.

Fortunately, however, as we discussed in Chapter 1, problems at any grade level — if the sources of the problems are accurately defined — can be dealt with appropriately and reasonably, opening the door to success.

What we teachers sometimes forget, however, is that what we learn about ourselves from how others treat us, however, can have as much impact — often more so — on whether or not we struggle than difficulty with a particular subject area.

Three of the most important things teachers bring to their students are acceptance, support and respect. Second only to family members, teachers are the most important "significant others" in children's lives. These three factors are essential to healthy emotional, social and intellectual development.

Unfortunately, though, we seem to forget this, perhaps because when a student is struggling in school, it is one of the most difficult and frustrating experiences for all concerned. A child may become defiant, act out or refuse to do classwork. He may lie, to himself, his parents and his teachers about homework, projects, reports or almost anything school-related, to make himself feel better or to get his parents and teachers off his back.

At the same time, many children with problems in school who do none of that. They work hard — some even *too* hard — and are respectful, but yet struggle to get an A, B or C.

How do these kids get over the hurdles and succeed, while others don't? Because they are lucky to have adults in their lives who work with them to pinpoint their problems and help them deal with them. Their teachers accept them where they are, no matter how limited or advanced. They support these children — never walking away and throwing up their arms in disgust when grades slip.

Perhaps most important, they respect the child's efforts to achieve, no matter how modest the successes. They understand and remember that no one *wants* to fail.

Every student wants the gold star, the A+, the 100% and chances are, although a kid sitting behind the desk doesn't seem to care, in reality, she is more likely confused, frightened, ashamed.

Understanding the STRONG Learning Model

Where the Common Core State Standards measure student knowledge/skill outcomes, the STRONG Learning Model goes further — effectively addressing critical facets of the classroom climate that, ignored, tend to impede, if not completely thwart students' successes.

The importance of the quality of classroom instruction and command of pedagogy is a no-brainer. The CCSS are standards of factual and conceptual knowledge that will impact the ease with which today's students will enter and contribute in the global workplace and society in general. And student test scores are the most obvious surface level measurements of teacher effectiveness. There is no doubt that good teachers in positive learning situations have a positive impact on student test scores or that student test scores are often negatively impacted by poor teachers. But the definition of a "good" teacher doesn't stop at mastery of content and pedagogy.

Research has shown over and over that the children who perform best in school are their *own* advocates with respect to learning and achievement, independent of the quality of classroom instruction. As with Michael, with whose story we began this chapter, there are countless examples of students who excel despite myriad factors beyond their control, from learning dysfunctions to poverty to family problems to the teacher they're assigned to.

Why? Because they know that their teachers are their *allies*, not their adversaries. During our school years, our identities form and develop, laying the foundation for who we will become and how effective we will be in achieving success in life. This means that we, as teachers have tremendous power over not just what our students learn about the subject matter we teach, but about how they come to view *themselves.*

With great power comes great responsibility. Fortunately, as you will see, the components of a healthy identity are also the very same nutrients our classroom environments must supply in order for learning to take place.

STRONG is an acronym, its letters representing the components of a healthy identity and the life skills we need to maintain a healthy identity throughout life:

THE STRONG MODEL

S	**SELF-ESTEEM.** Self-esteem is a measure of our personal worth and ability. Positive self-esteem plays a central role in good character as it serves as a template that directly or indirectly influences who we are and what we do. Interestingly, self-esteem is based on the perception, whether accurate or not, of how the significant others in our lives view and value us and how we view and value ourselves, and the extent to which we perceive that we measure up to the standards thus created.
T	**TRUST.** Trust plays a pivotal role in social connectedness, thus it is a pillar of positive self-esteem. Self-esteem is nurtured in an environment of trust. First we learn to trust our significant others and later to become trustworthy ourselves.
R	**RESPONSIBILITY.** The foundation of trust is the tangible evidence that we do what we are responsible for doing and can count on others to do the same. Becoming responsible to ourselves, our significant others and those in our community is a pillar of positive self-esteem. So too is taking responsibility for and being proactive in molding our future.
O	**OPTIONS.** The ability to make good decisions requires that we know there are different ways to achieve the same results and have the skill to choose the options that give us the highest probability of success. As we experience success in decision-making, our self-esteem is enhanced.
N	**NEEDS.** To function at our best, our brains and bodies must have nutritious food, sufficient sleep, physically and emotionally safe environments and time to relax and recharge. If those needs aren't met or we are unable to meet them ourselves, our self-esteem suffers.
G	**GOALS.** Goals are like rudders on ships. Whether short- or long-term, they keep us pointed in the direction we need to go to get to our destination—success. Confidence that we have the ability to set goals, assess our movement toward them, and achieve them, is central to the development and maintenance of self-esteem.

The STRONG Learning Model leads with self-esteem because, in addition to being the central focus of identity development, everything else in the model hinges on and contributes to the development and maintenance of healthy self-esteem.

Trust is next, because healthy self-esteem can only be developed in an environment of trust — an environment where the powerful people in our lives have earned our confidence that they will do what they say and provide a model for how to be trustworthy ourselves. Being responsible is the tangible demonstration of that trustworthiness.

The remaining parts of the STRONG model relate to knowledge and skills humans need in everyday life — how to make good decisions, take care of ourselves physically and emotionally, and set and achieve goals important to our success in school, the workplace and society in general.

We believe that, in its purest form, our classrooms are small microcosms that imitate life, and that, like academic knowledge, life skills are more easily (and safely) learned and practiced there. In the following chapters, we will examine each of the STRONG components in greater detail with case studies, explanations and suggestions for how to give students the practice they need to become adults of good character and help them acquire the academic skills and knowledge they will need to succeed — *at the same time.*

Chapter 5

Self-Esteem

**"Oh, her. She always gets 100's. She's so smart.
I'm not — I'm one of the dumb girls."**

— Lily, Age 12 —

Lily was an adorable 7th grader. She viewed school as a place where there are smart kids and dumb kids — and she saw herself as one of the dumb kids. It was almost like a caste system. She said that all the brainy, popular kids sat at one side of the lunchroom and all the dumb, unpopular kids sat at other tables. She sat at the other tables.

"What makes them the popular girls?" I asked her.

"They all get 100's and the teachers always talk to them and call on them. They're perfect," said Lily.

She continued. "You know what I'm doing? I'm writing a book about the girls I sit with. I'll show the other girls that we're just as smart as they are."

Lilly provided one anecdote after another to support her "case."

Lily's situation is as common today as it has been for decades. She lacks confidence in her abilities and since she's not in the "A-List" group at school, her self-esteem is impacted. In talking with Lily, it seems her teacher tells her that she just needs to study more, her mom tells her that she's just as smart as those other girls and her dad tells her that she's just lazy. She's getting mixed messages.

Lily is in a situation that is difficult for her because she doesn't quite know who she is or where she fits in. Her teacher may be right—perhaps Lily doesn't know how to study well. If this is the case, her teacher needs to help her develop strategies that will improve those skills.

Then again, her mom may be right. Lily may be just as smart as the other girls, but she needs to help Lily sort out what might be causing her to do poorly.

Lily's father needs to do the same without being judgmental. When a parent or teacher says that a student is "lazy," I always correct them and say, "Perhaps she isn't interested in the subject or it may be one that's difficult for her." (Sometimes I suggest that it might be the adult who is "lazy," if they haven't taken the time to discover the real reason why the child is struggling in school.)

Without her parents and teachers helping to discover why Lily is struggling with school, she may always feel like a failure and have low self-esteem.

Promoting Self-Esteem

It takes time, energy, caring and a clear understanding of the components that promote self-esteem to raise a healthy, self-assured child. If you want to mentor a child to be emotionally and socially healthy, then building self-esteem is the key. Its importance cannot be overstated—self-esteem is an indispensable aspect of human growth and development both in school and out.

There is a distinction, however, between genuine self-esteem and inflated self-esteem, as demonstrated in the following story:

The Mouse and the Psychiatrist

To overcome his fear of cats, a mouse consulted a mouse psychiatrist. The psychiatrist reassured the mouse, telling him that he was a strong and mighty animal who need not give in to his fear.

The mouse continued his visits, week after week, where he was praised for his strength and ability. After the final session, now feeling really good about himself, the mouse departed.

No sooner did he leave, when along came a cat, who…well…*you* know what happened. (Gulp!)

The moral? A mouse that is all puffed up is still a mouse. The psychiatrist did not have to tell the mouse he was a weakling or a coward, but she should have encouraged him to acquire the skills necessary to avoid a marauding cat. The mouse could then have felt proud of himself for his accomplishments and he would have developed genuine self-esteem. Instead, his ego was inflated to the point where it distorted his view of himself and the realities of the world in which he lived.

Seven Essential Factors For Development of High Self-Esteem in Children

1. Perceiving they are *accepted* and will be *supported* by their significant others (parents, teachers and peers)
2. Believing their most important significant others *like* them and think they're great
3. Feeling *safe,* physically and emotionally
4. Feeling part of a family, school and community
5. Feeling *respected* by their significant others and in turn, showing respect to them
6. Having logical boundaries
7. Having parents with high self-esteem

Supporting and Accepting Your Students for Who They Are

"I'm really good in social studies. I love my teacher. I always get A's. I hate math — I have a 42 average! My teacher *hates* me."

— Jessica, Age 14 —

It's an interesting phenomenon that when students like their teachers and they perceive their teachers like them, they'll work for those teachers and do well. They'll feel good about themselves, too. When they get an A, they own it. They don't say, "My teacher helped me." Instead, they are proud to say, "I got an A."

On the other hand, when a student does poorly in a subject, like Jessica, suddenly it's the teacher's fault. "He hates me." No child wants to feel that she's "stupid" or not capable of succeeding, so she'll blame the teacher instead. Her self-confidence impacted, she is less likely to accept ownership of her lower grades.

Teachers are right up there in importance and influence, coming in second behind their parents. As one of our students' most important significant others, what we do and say affects how our students feel about themselves.

During the elementary grades, starting around ages seven and eight, a child starts to form identity. They think concretely: *I am tall or I am short, I am fat or I am skinny, I am poor or I am rich, I am smart or I am dumb.* Teachers, along with parents and peers, are a formidable presence that help to create a child's self-image, an image that may be with her for the rest of her life.

As the child develops and enters middle school, her peer group becomes increasingly important in how she feels about herself: *This one likes me, but that one doesn't; I'm in the "in" group; or I'm in the outside group "looking in" at the popular kids.* This continues right through high school. Teachers who embarrass or humiliate a child at any point in the school experience, e.g., by announcing a poor grade in front of the class, telling her to leave the room, comparing him to another student, inadvertently create wounds to self-esteem that stay with the child forever. A teacher's words and actions are sometimes imprinted in a student's memory.

Just think back to when you were in school. You may not remember when you learned that there are seven continents in the world, but you probably remember if a teacher embarrassed you or a fellow classmate.

> **When you speak, a student may perceive messages you don't even know you're sending.**

Self-Esteem Grows Through Words and Actions: Let Your Students Know You Think They're Great!

You may not have realized how important it is to be aware of what you say and how you speak to your students. Are your comments constructive or destructive? What does your face look like when you speak? How does your voice sound? What does your body language convey?

It is not uncommon for students to perceive messages teachers don't even know they're sending.

The way our students think we view them — even if we say otherwise or their perceptions are wrong — impacts the way they begin to view themselves. If children believe that their significant others value them, they are more likely to feel worthy. Genuinely feeling valued is critical to their emotional development and school success.

Perceptions are judgments. They are highly subjective and based on hunches, opinions, gestures and other subtle actions. Students can easily misinterpret messages from their teachers — so we need to be sure we don't unwittingly send them unintended messages.

Offhand comments made to others that a child overhears, like, "Oh, him. *He's* not going anywhere," or a "look" exchanged between you and an assistant that a child sees, often says more to a student about your opinion of him than what you say to his face. You may only be joking with the assistant, but some children aren't mature enough to place your comments in context. They may "hear" an underlying negative message even though it's not intended. Self-confidence is all about perception.

Picture going into a room where everybody likes you and thinks you're the smartest or funniest person they ever met. You feel great. You're relaxed. You're happy to participate and be part of the group.

Now, picture entering a room where you perceive that you're thought of as stupid, lazy, too fat or too thin, not dressed appropriately, boring, or "the one who talks too much."

Would you be willing to participate? Or would you wish there were a hole in the floor to crawl into? How would you respond? Sit there and say nothing? Become sarcastic, aggressive or belligerent? What reactions would your behavior communicate to others in the room?

One thing's for certain — whatever your response, it would be based on your *perception* of what others thought of you, which could be accurate — or not.

Perception affects your relationship with your students, too. If a student perceives that you don't like her, accept her, or support her, her feeling of self-worth will suffer and with it, her motivation. As a result, she may shut down in class or she may stop doing homework or preparing for tests.

We, as teachers, set the climate for our classes. It is crucial that we be aware of the "messages" we are sending to our students and mindful of how our students perceive themselves through our eyes.

Use Language That Builds Self-Esteem

"There is no way I'm going to be humiliated again."

—Tom, Age 17—

Tom was a teenager with severe dyslexia and dysgraphia. I worked with Tom on his reading and writing skills; the school helped him with homework and other subjects.

A bright, gregarious teen who had high aspirations for himself, Tom loved talking to anyone who came into our office and thought nothing of walking over to see if he could help a younger child. He had even attained the highest level in scouting—he was an Eagle Scout.

One day in May, Tom asked if I could help him make up work for his history class. I asked him what was happening and he pulled out a paper he had written in February. It was the first time he had the courage to test his wings and try to do an assignment on his own.

There was a big red "X" covering the paper. Compared with what unimpaired students produce, his paper was admittedly shabby, but it was a breakthrough achievement for Tom. He explained that his teacher had returned the paper to him and said, in a loud voice, "Don't think you're handing this in for credit. This is totally unacceptable! That's another zero for you."

Crestfallen, Tom walked back to his seat. For the next three months, he had sat in the class with his back to the wall and done absolutely nothing. He had not handed in another assignment.

Knowing what I did about Tom, I would have had the opposite reaction from that of his teacher. I would have been delighted to see an actual paragraph that he had written by himself. Because of his disabilities, writing a paragraph — even though there were countless spelling errors — was a monumental achievement. It took courage — no, it took *guts*.

But instead of recognizing the positive, the teacher had unnecessarily embarrassed him in front of his classmates. What happened here? Tom's teacher's response to the paper was not a perception, but a reality. Yes, it was far beneath an 11th grader's work, but, for Tom, it was a true accomplishment. His response to her negative evaluation was to protect himself — in his mind, if he didn't do anything else in class, he couldn't be humiliated.

To try and set things right, I spoke to Tom's teacher. It was clear that she had misinterpreted Tom's behavior as lazy and defiant. She was unaware of how her response had broken his spirit, but the damage had been done. The details are not important to include, but somehow we managed to salvage the year so he didn't have to repeat the course.

> **The manner in which you speak to your students can profoundly affect their self-esteem.**

You're the grown up. The manner in which you speak to your students can promote or diminish their self-esteem.

Following are examples of phrases you can use to encourage students having a challenge with their studies that can help to build self-esteem:

- "What a great idea!"
- "That was a good try."
- "I'm proud to be your teacher."
- "I always knew you could do it!"
- "I can depend on you to try and if you still find it difficult, you'll come to me for help. You never give up."

Again, use *your* experiences to determine what to do or not do as a teacher. Think of a time when *you* were put down, harshly criticized, called names, or cursed at by workmates, spouse, children, family, or peers. How did you feel? Did you hurry to correct your behavior? Probably not! Chances are you withdrew or became angry and resentful.

When a student does something that needs to be corrected, use words that promote growth and self-esteem. Constructive criticism stresses positive points and suggests improvements. It doesn't cut a child down; instead, it builds him up while acknowledging there is still work to be done.

Negative statements, on the other hand, can harm self-esteem. They create ill feelings, unnecessary confrontations or stalemates and can sometimes give rise to antisocial behaviors. They stimulate some students — like Tom — to throw in the towel altogether.

Avoid statements like these:

- "You're always trying to get away with something."
- "Let's not be stupid."
- "That's just one more zero."
- "I didn't think you would study."
- "How are you ever going to amount to anything?"

Similarly, avoid using sarcasm:

- "Okay, genius, let's see how you'll do on this test."
- "Yeah, right. *You're* going to college!"

Sarcastic remarks are transparent ways of putting someone down and, if they're directed toward your students, they know it.

Have you ever been sarcastic with a student? Did it accomplish what you wanted it to, *i.e.,* did he learn? Did the student change his behavior because of the criticism? Probably not. And even if his behavior *did* change, it may well have been out of fear of your disapproval — not because he understood what he was doing wrong.

When you see a student struggling, there's a reason. Until you know what it is, be mindful of what you say and how you say it. Instead of being reactive, seek to be positive and proactive in your language and your tone.

Children use us as mirrors. If we think and convey to them that they are wonderful, they will think and believe that they are wonderful and they'll work hard for us. If we think and tell them they are stupid, they will think and believe they are incapable of achievement.

Instead of...	Try...
"I'm not accepting that," and throwing the paper in the trashcan or tearing it up.	"This is a great starting point. Try to print it a little neater and add one more sentence. Then let me look at it again."
"You call that a story? It's three sentences long, for crying out loud!"	"Your choice of words is perfect. Let's see if your story has a beginning, a middle and an end. What do you think?"
"How are you going to get better at reading if you don't even try?"	"You read that sentence so well. How did you know those words?"
"You're just careless. You could have all the correct answers but you didn't even try!"	"I noticed you missed many of these problems. Maybe you rushed through it. Here's a way to slow yourself down. It works for a lot of kids whose hand goes faster than they can think."
"Stop talking to your friends! That's why you're never going to get out of school!"	"You have a great gift of gab. I admire you for that. Unfortunately, it's hard to run a class when everyone is talking. Let's take a few minutes at the end of class to just talk to each other."

The King and His Sons

One rainy day, the king took a walk with his two children. He held an umbrella in each hand to cover and protect each child. A bystander approached and asked, "Why are you protecting your children from the rain? You are the king! They should be protecting you."

His Highness sagely replied, "If I do not show them respect, how will they learn to respect me? How will they learn to respect others? How will they learn to respect themselves?"

To Earn Respect, Show Respect

Treat your students as you expect to be treated. When children are treated with respect, they learn to respect themselves and others. The ancient tale presented on the facing page provides a perfect illustration of the role teachers play when showing and teaching respect. *Genuine respect promotes self-respect.*

Be Open and Available

Are you approachable? Does your body language tell your students you don't want to be bothered? Or does it communicate that you will listen if they have questions or problems?

Of course, there are times when you are in the midst of a lesson or doing something for the benefit of the whole class and can't stop to attend to one student's immediate needs. But, if you have a free moment during a break or after class, follow up with a student who requests your help. Demonstrate that you are someone students can count on to talk to if a need arises.

If a student perceives that a teacher is too busy, disinterested, or annoyed to listen, then her problems, no matter how trivial they may seem to adults, may overwhelm her. Just knowing you're there and ready to listen without judgment provides students with comfort and security.

Recognize and Applaud Effort

It's easy to give kudos to students who ace their work, but what about the student who fails a test or turns in an unsatisfactory paper or homework assignment? For the average or failing student, it isn't the instructional *outcome* that begs acknowledgment—a student's effort should be recognized, too, because it encourages him to persist. (For high-achieving students, the feedback of the grade itself motivates.)

Avoid being patronizing, however. Strive to be realistic and genuine with your praise—children *know* when they do well *and* when they don't. False praise is insulting.

> **The bottom line: Give your students the kind of respect you expect from them.**

Be Understanding of Your Student's Personal Problems

When you see that a student isn't engaged in class or is acting out, take a few minutes during the day to ask how she feels and listen attentively to what she says. Instead of asking general questions about school activities, you could try "drawing out" your student to see if there are any personal problems of which you are unaware. For example, instead of asking, "Why didn't you read along with the class today?" you might ask, "Is something upsetting you? I noticed you seem preoccupied and haven't been participating in class for a few days."

If a student tells you what's bothering him, you may want to offer help or suggest alternative strategies, such as after-school assistance. If despite obvious problems the answer is, "I'm okay" or a child doesn't answer at all, contact the parents to share your concerns. Let them know that you've seen a change in their child's behavior.

If you see something you believe to be a serious problem, don't try to shoulder the entire burden yourself. Seek help from your school's psychologist or guidance counselor. They're trained for this purpose and are great resources.

Initiate Activities That Involve Creating and Doing

Working on a creative level stimulates one of the highest forms of intellectual growth. By creating and carrying out projects on their own, children learn to plan, organize, cooperate and evaluate. The importance of activities like these often gets lost when you're already challenged to get through the curriculum, but they are the very skills needed to succeed in school — and in life as well.

Try to Forgive Forgetfulness

Let's face it. It's common for children to be forgetful. The same is true for many adults — that's why we carry laptop computers, daily planners, tablets and smartphones, or hire efficient support personnel to keep us on schedule.

When an adult forgets, we attribute it to a stressful and preoccupied life, yet we often can't see that the same explanation is true for children. In the midst of our own struggles, we fail to realize how stressful their lives may be.

So when a child slips up once in a while, it's only natural. Instead of jumping all over a forgetful child, help her set up methods of support so that she will remember her assignments and responsibilities more easily.

Berating a child over absentmindedness does not help her to learn and it shows a lack of respect. A reprimand like "You forgot your homework again. I don't want to hear any excuses," not only won't achieve the outcome you desire but is hurtful to a student. It does nothing to create an environment conducive to learning. It destroys it.

If a student *habitually* forgets things, work with him to find strategies to help him develop new habits. There is no demonstrated relationship between giving out one zero after another or keeping a young child in from recess for a month and improvements to absentmindedness. Be understanding, supportive and persist in finding creative strategies that work for the individual child.

—Mark, Age 19—

Mark was attending community college when I first met him. He was failing his classes, but not because he couldn't do the work — he just didn't do it. He even forgot to go to class. This was nothing new for Mark as he always had organizational and time management issues. Since Mark depended on his smartphone for all his communication, we devised a way to put all his classes and assignments on the device.

But, the next time we met, he had forgotten to take his phone to school. Why? It was charging at home. I asked him where he usually kept his phone and he replied that he kept it in his jacket pocket.

Ta-da! Problem solved. From that day on, Mark developed the habit of putting his jacket on the floor next to the outlet where his phone was being charged. After that, he got to all his classes and completed all his assignments on time — until spring arrived and Mark didn't need his jacket anymore.

What did we do then? We came up with another strategy.

Control Your Anger

Many teachers become so frustrated with their students that the frustration morphs into anger. Some even wind up lashing out verbally. When you feel yourself getting progressively more angry with a student, or the whole class, keep this in mind: If you respect someone, do you yell at or insult him? Verbal attacks against students show blatant disregard for their rights and you come off looking bad. You also send the wrong message—that it is okay to act on your feelings when, in fact, your goal is to teach students to think first—and think clearly—before they act.

Be a Good Role Model

You can't teach what you don't know. Children have a better chance of developing high self-esteem when those closest to them, primarily their parents and then their teachers, demonstrate high self-esteem. Children learn to value themselves (or not to) from modeled behavior.

What they observe you doing influences your students' character far more than what you say. If you exude confidence, you pass on those traits to your students by example. If, on the other hand, you are unhappy with your job, are depressed, or are verbally self-deprecating, the environment in your classroom will not be one that is conducive to learning or developing self-esteem.

Obviously, the emotional byproducts of a stressful life must be dealt with. But in the classroom, as a professional educator, *you are the adult.* Your stress is not the focus here. Be mindful of the impact of your actions and behavior so that your students can grow from your example and learn how to deal with life's curveballs in a responsible and healthy way.

Suggestions for Promoting *Your* Self-Esteem

- Share your original ideas, opinions and thoughts with peers and faculty members. Don't just take on the ideas and opinions of others.
- Don't just talk — take action. Show your students that you are a doer, not just a talker.
- Respond to feedback. Don't automatically consider what others say to be more — or less — important than what you have to say. Listen, reflect and respond appropriately.
- Set realistic short- and long-term goals for yourself. What do you hope to accomplish this year? In ten years? What kind of teacher would you like to be? How can you make that happen?
- Attend to your personal needs: Eat well, get plenty of sleep, exercise and be sure to leave some time for fun.
- Sort out your options so that you can make appropriate decisions. Recognize that you have the capacity to help determine your destiny and not let others determine it for you.
- Work toward becoming competent in one or more areas in addition to your own specialty. As a teacher, you always have to stay current in your field — expanding your knowledge keeps your mind active and your expertise growing. Pursuing and mastering outside interests can keep you well-balanced.

Help Kids Feel That They Are Part of the School Community

"I don't want to go to school. I hate school."
— Alexis, Age 10 —

*Alexis had just moved to a new house and school. As a newcomer, she had trouble gaining acceptance from the other girls in class. When her teacher learned that Alexis loved horses, she brought her a copy of **Black Beauty**.*

She explained to Alexis that this was a classic book that she had read and loved as a child. Alexis started reading the book and shared her progress with her teacher. Their discussions only took a few minutes a day, but to Alexis it meant the world. She felt her teacher cared about her and, in turn, she wanted to please her teacher.

Soon after, another student asked about the book and then another. When interest in the book continued to increase, the teacher asked everyone in class if they had read it. A few had, but several others said they wanted to read it.

Why would children *volunteer* to read an unassigned book? *They wanted to be part of something special.*

Many children are uncomfortable at school, are shy, or have trouble fitting in. As a result, they often have difficulty concentrating in class and hesitate to seek help, join clubs and attend after-school events. This difficulty in adapting to change often happens when a student moves from one state or town to another or when transferring to a different school in the same area. As one recently transplanted 16-year-old told me, "I always feel as if everyone is wearing black shoes and I'm wearing brown."

Abraham Maslow theorized that as humans get older, we need to feel we belong not only in our *families*, but also in broader groups. School introduces children to an important new community. School personnel, especially teachers, do well to focus on fostering a sense of community for the students in their classes and at their school.

Suggestions for Helping Your Students Feel a Sense of Belonging in Your Class and School

- If you see a child has difficulty joining in, introduce her to another child who may become a friend.
- If a child shows interests in a particular sport, musical instrument, artistic pursuit, or debate, encourage him to join the associated school club. If there's no club to join, encourage him to start one.
- Have a shy child or a new student having difficulty volunteer to help a teacher or kids in a lower grade.
- Have a special day in your class or school. For example, have your students wear their clothes backwards or come to school in their PJs, where the "rules" apply to everyone.
- Have a pot luck dinner for your class. Arrange a weeknight for kids to come to school with their families and have each family bring a favorite dish. This is particularly fun in a multi-cultural area.

Note: *In planning activities, take care to consider the economic circumstances of all the children in your classroom. Avoid those requiring extra expenditures – you may expose a vulnerable child to unnecessary embarrassment.*

Second to parents, teachers are among children's most important significant others. If you genuinely accept, support and respect your students and it shows through your words and actions, you sow the seeds of genuine self-esteem. If a child doesn't feel important, no matter how intelligent he may be, he's unlikely to exert the effort to reach his full potential.

Chapter 6

Trust

**"I wouldn't go to any of my teachers.
They're all idiots."**

— Ben, Age 14 —

Ben had many learning disabilities and was a year older than his classmates because he had been retained in first grade.

The first time Ben came to my office, he was defiant, angry and scared. His mom stood next to him and spoke for him. If I asked him a question, she jumped in before Ben could even think of an answer.

"Do you know why you're here?" I asked Ben.

His mom interrupted. "I told him that you'll teach him how to study."

"Ben," I said looking directly at him, "why do you think you're here?"

"I don't know. You'll help me in math? I don't know," said Ben as he looked around the room. It was obvious that he didn't want to be there.

I assured Ben that I didn't care if he got 100's or zeroes because I didn't have a refrigerator with fruit-shaped magnets on which to post his grades. He still just sat without responding. I told him that my only job was to help him learn how to learn, so he could get out of high school and go on to the career of his choice. I also told him that while he was working with me, his parents would not be allowed to ground him or punish him over school issues.

"Yeah, right. Like SHE's going to listen."

"I get mad because you don't put in any effort," said Ben's mother. "I told you that if I saw some effort I'd give you back some privileges. But I can't trust you. You promise me that you're going to do all your homework and study for your tests, but you do nothing. You always say, 'Trust me,' but I can't."

Ben fumed. "I stayed after school for math help the other day, but my teacher didn't show up. That's not my fault! I did what I had to do and you didn't give me back anything."

Trust was apparently a problem at home and at school. Though Ben's mother said she wanted what was best for him and his teachers likely said the same, Ben didn't perceive that he could trust them.

Mom had forgotten the importance of role modeling. To regain her son's trust, she needed to show trust in him. She said that she understood the need to be calm and helpful, but when she saw Ben's grades and was confronted with his attitude, she invariably acted on her emotions.

On top of all that, Ben's mom and dad had recently divorced and he hadn't seen much of his father.

> **What children learn at home often manages to find its way *outside* the home — especially at school.**

How did Ben react to his perception of a lack of trustworthiness at home and school? He learned to talk back, to lie, to do anything he could to avoid punishment and not suffer a loss of self-esteem. I asked Ben how he treated the teachers at school, knowing that if he was rude to them, they were probably reacting to it.

> *"Perhaps the math teacher didn't meet you after school because he didn't trust that you'd be there."*
> *"No! He's just an idiot!"*
> *"Have you ever been rude to your science teacher?"*
> *"Only when she was rude to me,"* he answered defiantly.

I asked Ben to imagine inviting 25 kids to his house for a Saturday night party and then asked him, "What if on the night of the party, most of the kids arrive late? What if some refuse to go along with any of the planned activities? What if others talk while you're trying to tell a joke or ignores everyone and falls asleep in a chair. How would you feel?

"That's what *teachers* go through," I told him. "Every day they plan what they hope will be a pleasant lesson — sort of like a party — and they feel pretty upset and sometimes downright angry, when some kids in the class ruin everything by being uncooperative or rude or even by going to sleep."

It took some time, but Ben finally got the point. And once both his mother and I demonstrated that *we* were trustworthy, he began to respond in kind.

Connecting Trust and Trustworthiness

An environment conducive to learning requires mutual trust between teachers and their students *and* mutual trust between parents and their children.

From infancy on, children need to be able to trust others. The development of trust starts with their earliest caregivers, when they learn that their earliest cries of hunger and discomfort will bring attention and relief. From a protective and nurturing home environment, the number of trusting relationships branches out from there.

The other dimension of mutual trust — *trustworthiness* — develops later. It has to be learned. The best, if not only, ways of facilitating trustworthiness in children is by example. Only when *you* are trustworthy can you rationally demand trustworthiness from another. Teachers need to "show up" when they say they will, both literally and figuratively, for their students.

Improving school and family relationships that have become deficient in trust is hard work for everyone involved. It takes time and patience, especially if the trust issues stem from circumstances at home. This makes your trustworthiness all the more important to the child in question.

How to Promote Trust In Your Students

- *Be consistent.* If you behave unpredictably, your students will learn to be wary of you instead of trusting you. Don't, for example, tell them that there will be a test on Friday and then change it to another day without warning or apology, unless there is a very good reason to do so.

- *Keep grades and assessments confidential.*
- *Never announce grades in class.* If you must post them, use a code only the student knows.
- *Until students give you a reason not to, use the honor system.* Give your students an opportunity to demonstrate their trustworthiness.
- *Match expectations for behavior to your students' ages and maturation level.* "Failing" at something you aren't capable of doing is downright demoralizing.
- *Put yourself in your students' shoes.* Don't do things that are adversarial, such as springing tests on them just after winter break. They need the same readjustment time that you do.

Be Communicative and Compassionate

Even if it's just for a few minutes each day, talk to your students about how they're doing in school, about homework you've given, or about general events relevant to their lives. If you know someone's parent or grandparent is ill, ask how he or she is doing. Ask about the new dog or baby at home. After a holiday break, discuss what everyone did on their vacations. Look for ways to continue to build on the trusting relationship you have with your students.

Let your students know from the very first day of school that you are on their team and that if they need help, they'll get it.

On Lying

Lying is often a symptom of a lack of trust. In the school setting, lying is often employed by children to conceal from teachers and parents that they are having trouble in school.

We're convinced that lying is all about *perceived* consequences. (There's that word again.) Here's what we mean. To kids, the consequences of being caught in a lie are often less severe than those they believe they'll face if they tell the truth. For them, the consequences for lying are often more predictable (and less potentially damaging to self-esteem) than the remedies some teachers devise to try to solve problems with learning.

For example, to kids with learning disabilities especially, recopying an entire paper just because it is too messy is torture, as is correcting 20 math problems or looking up 30 misspelled words. It's like being required to watch a foreign film over and over when you don't speak the language.

So, when you are next confronted with what you know is a lie, consider the possibility that you aren't dealing with an issue of a student's trustworthiness at all. Consider that lying may simply be a sign that a child is having trouble and needs you to help him devise a way to overcome his unique obstacles while undergirding his self-esteem.

Classroom Issues that Diminish Trust

There are many issues that can make some children feel unsafe. Here are some important, but not always obvious issues that sometimes arise in the classroom.

Fear of embarrassment

The threat of embarrassment and humiliation is an issue for children and adults alike, but the events that aren't even slightly anxiety-producing for some may be paralyzing for others. Some have such fear of being embarrassed that they are unable to function in school, much less achieve.

Samantha, a fifth grader, confided to me that she listens in class but doesn't always understand what the teacher is saying. The reason? She has a severe auditory processing problem. Above average intelligence helps her get by, but she faces this conundrum on a continuing basis. She's afraid to ask the teacher because she's been accused of not listening, but she can't ask a friend sitting next to her to explain, because she's afraid she'll be reprimanded for talking.

Samantha is not alone. This happens to everybody at some time in their academic lives. Parents easily see this point when I ask them if they raise their hands and ask questions in large lecture halls. They look at me as if I've lost my mind.

Consider establishing a "memo box" where students can drop anonymous notes about things that are troubling them at school—a bully, an academic subject, a homework assignment, or anything else of concern. This provides a safe and confidential way for students to communicate with their teachers while avoiding potential embarrassment.

Concerns about missing recess

Recess is just plain fun, not to mention an opportunity to expend extra energy that often finds its way into acting out. Kids need and look forward to having this break, so withholding recess as a punishment for difficulty with academic work is detrimental to their physical and emotional wellbeing.

—Travis, age 7—

Travis, a second-grader, said, "I'm afraid I'll have to sit at the wall."

Not sure what he meant, I asked for more details.

It seemed that anyone who wasn't finished with the morning's work by time for recess was required to sit at a school desk, facing a brick wall, to continue doing their classwork while the others played.

Travis processes information slowly and because of it, he wasn't able to keep up. In spite of the fact that his learning disability had been identified, it seemed he had been required to sit with other children who were being punished for bad behavior.

I asked Travis who his teacher was and was shocked. It turned out that his *current* teacher didn't use the "wall" as a disciplinary action. It had been his teacher the year before! In spite of the fact that his work had been modified and he was allowed extended time to compensate for his learning disability, the anxiety he felt because of his previous teacher's actions had lingered.

While Travis's situation is fortunately both uncommon and extreme, recess is, again, a time when kids can have fun, expend energy and rejuvenate. Avoid withholding it as a method of punishment in general and especially if you are uninformed with respect to all of the issues affecting a child in your class.

Fear over being left or held back

Without realizing it, parents and teachers create unnecessary fear in children when they threaten them with the specter of repeating a grade. Children are afraid of being held back because of the humiliation they have seen others experience as a result of it.

Yet, in attempts to "prod" children who are performing below average to work harder, well-meaning parents and teachers often use this threat as a "motivating" tool. In the more recent years of high-stakes testing, we've even heard of children being told that if they don't pass state assessment tests, they'll be held back as well.

As a result, some children work themselves into frenzies taking the state tests and, as a result of self-fulfilling prophecy, do, indeed, end up performing poorly. The question remains as to whether we're testing academic achievement or the capacity to manage anxiety.

When poor academic performance begins to create high anxiety in students, it's time to work with parents and school personnel to assess what is happening and why and take positive measures to support and supplement learning so that the probability of a student's success is enhanced. One thing's for sure—at times like this, idle threats are counterproductive.

The Importance of Rules in Establishing an Environment of Trust

We all need rules—children and adults alike. Rules serve as boundaries to establish what is and is not acceptable behavior, especially in group settings. Parents begin setting boundaries for their children from the time they are born.

Teachers set rules for their classrooms. Rules are necessary, but to be effective in achieving their purposes, the rules need to be well-thought-out, relevant to the situation, logical in their intent and fair to all involved, or they can backfire.

— Amy, Age 8 —

Amy rarely finished her class work and what she did finish was done shabbily. Her mom couldn't understand why her teacher referred to her as a "problem student," so she brought her to me for an evaluation. The teacher explained, "I have my rules and Amy needs to follow them."

Early in the session I asked Amy what happened when the teacher told the class to do something. Amy replied, "When the teacher tells us what to do, she talks so fast, I don't know what she says."

I asked Amy why she didn't ask the teacher to repeat herself or for help. "We're not allowed to do that," Amy responded. "The teacher says, 'You gotta ask three, then me.'"

"What does that mean?" I asked.

"We have to ask three kids what we're supposed to do before we are allowed to ask the teacher," she replied. "I used to do that, but the kids I asked acted annoyed and stopped answering me. They started calling me stupid."

My testing revealed that Amy had a language processing problem. She was telling the truth—she simply didn't understand the teacher's verbal or written instructions or those of the children who were kind enough to attempt to help her. She needed directions given in multiple ways—

explained to her, then shown to her and then, if necessary, communicated through some other method.

I sent a copy of my report to her teacher and discussed with her the impact of her rule on Amy's disability. She adjusted it to better accommodate Amy's unique situation and things improved thereafter.

Avoid Making Arbitrary Rules

While some rules work well for the majority of children, with others they may be ineffective. In addition, many teachers establish rules based only on their own needs or convenience without considering that the rules may not be appropriate for some or all of their students.

In Amy's case, her teacher understandably didn't want to be barraged with a million unnecessary questions, so she established the "ask three, then me" rule. Admittedly, it's a cute rhyme and easy to remember, but for Amy, who couldn't understand what her teacher was saying because of a language processing issue, the rule had unintended consequences. One little boy admitted to me that when he didn't understand what the teacher wanted him to do, he went to the bathroom and stayed there until that part of the lesson was over. Another child often feigned illness and went to see the school nurse.

Be sure your rules make sense. No matter your intent when creating a rule, make sure that its rationale is something that makes sense to your students, too. "Because I said so" or "Because this is my classroom" won't do.

With young children, begin with the basic cause-and-effect logic behind some common rules. For example, ask the question, "What would happen if everyone spoke at once?" Get all your students to start talking. After a minute of laughter and multiple conversations, have students offer explanations for why raising hands to speak when doing class work might be a good idea, or why there are rules about how to talk with classmates when working in groups. Naturally, there'll always be some who break the rules, but, hopefully, there'll be far fewer offenders.

Be sure that your rules are fair. Just as children should understand the purpose for a rule, they should be part of the rule-evaluation process as well. After sharing input with your students about one of your rules, you may have to do some serious soul-searching as you evaluate some of the questions that arise. Kids are quite good at poking holes in our best-laid plans. Did you establish the rule for your students' benefit or for your convenience? Unless you can kill both birds with one stone, rules that improve the learning environment should supersede individual convenience in the classroom.

Follow your own rules. One of the most difficult parts of this rule-establishing business is avoiding the temptation to "pull rank" and say, "I'm the teacher, so I can do whatever I want." While this is largely true, it sometimes creates a double standard, which always sets the stage for classroom discipline problems, disrupting the environment of mutual respect you may have worked hard to establish.

Years ago, I worked with Kathy, a 10th grader, who said, "Health is the dumbest class. The teacher is giving us all these reasons why we shouldn't smoke. I just passed her in her car and she was smoking! What's wrong with her? Why should we listen to her when she doesn't even do what she says?"

Whether we like it or not, actions do speak louder than words. If you're going to smoke, don't teach health. If you're going to have a rule that talking while your students do "seat work" will elicit an automatic zero, don't stand in the doorway talking to another teacher while they work. If your rule is "no texting during class," don't send your husband a message to bring home milk while your students are completing an assignment.

When a child breaks a rule, find out why. Sometimes teachers reprimand or punish children for breaking rules without first examining the myriad reasons why the rules might have been broken. Unfortunately, just asking children why they broke a rule doesn't work. Some children are so intimidated that they default to answering, "I don't know," which in turn, as often as not, "I don't know" results in punitive action or criticism too harsh for the situation.

A more effective way may be to ask the child to write down what happened and why he broke the rule. (This is not a time to be concerned about spelling, even if you're an English teacher.)

For a young child who can't yet write, calmly sit with him and discuss what happened. Talk about the reason you created the rule. Together, write down other ways he could have behaved rather than breaking the rule. Discuss how the rule could be changed so that it makes more sense. Remember your goal is to understand why the rule was broken and to make the reasons for the rule clearer so as to increase the likelihood that the rule isn't broken again for reasons other than obvious disobedience.

If your goal is to have a healthy class environment in which your students can learn what you're there to teach them, ensure your rules are fair and understood by all. When you establish them for your classroom, be sure that you observe them as well. Try not to assume you know the reasons a student may have broken a rule and punish based on your perception alone.

Safety Among Other Students

—Christopher, Age 11—

"Well, Christopher," I said enthusiastically, "in two weeks you start sixth grade and you'll be in middle school."

He burst into tears. "I don't want to go to middle school. I wish I c-c-could stay in my old school."

As I handed Christopher the box of tissues, I asked him why he was afraid to go to middle school.

His answer caught me by surprise. "I'm afraid the kids will grab me and put me in a locker and lock me in there," he said, still sobbing.

I found out later Christopher had seen this happen in a movie. He assumed it could happen to him.

Life imitates art, but art imitates life, too. There is no denying that excessive teasing and bullying is rampant in the schools. Stories about school violence make headlines with regularity. It's no wonder that some students worry that they may be the next targets.

Excessive Teasing or Bullying from Peers

Everyone experiences a little teasing during childhood, especially from siblings. And while most of us would have preferred to live without it, we usually managed to "brush it off." As a result, unfortunately, it is easy to expect children to do the same when they complain about being teased, or worse.

But today's teasing isn't necessarily the same. Just as they have had great impact on the methodologies of teaching, the evolving technologies and social media platforms offer insidious opportunities for harassment that are often difficult to trace and prevent. We need to prevent this hurtful behavior before it starts.

While learning to deal with teasing or bullying may be part of growing up, it makes children feel unsafe emotionally and physically and shouldn't be ignored. All children have the right to feel safe and accepted at school.

If a student complains or intimates that other kids are bothering him at school, don't ignore it. Observe the kids in question to determine if they are behaving disrespectfully or inappropriately toward others. Report what you see to your school counselor or principal—you may find that the same child or group has harassed other children too. By bringing this to the attention of school personnel, you can initiate getting the perpetrator the help he or she obviously needs, too.

Most states now have anti-bullying laws in place, so schools and teachers have resources that allow them to be more proactive than ever. If your school does not offer programs about bullying for parents and teachers, do what you can to get one implemented. Include lessons about it in your curriculum or involve the Parent-Teacher-Student organizations in your system. Excessive teasing or bullying is not harmless—it is a serious, even dangerous, form of harassment.

Conclusion

The first step to creating an environment in which students learn is the development of mutual trust. When students "know" that their teacher can be counted on to do what she says, and that she believes and trusts them too, they usually live up to their part of the bargain.

Chapter 7

Responsibility

—Troy, Age 12—

"Troy, you didn't hand in your essay," said his teacher.

"Oh, that's because I didn't know about it," replied Troy.

"Why didn't you know about it?"

"I was absent last week."

"You're still responsible to hand in your work," said the teacher.

"I was sick. I couldn't do anything," said Troy.

For Troy, this was to be an informal lesson in being responsible. He was about to learn that if he is absent, his responsibility for doing assigned work doesn't change but increases—that he now has the *added* responsibility of figuring out how to complete his assignments in spite of his absence, e.g., borrowing class notes from a friend or negotiating with his teacher for an extension of the deadline to complete the assignment.

A Burgeoning Sense of Responsibility is a Prerequisite for School Success

Being responsible is an essential element of good character. Learning to shoulder responsibility is an integral part of growth and development. Youngsters with genuine self-esteem and a sense of responsibility to themselves and others are more likely to succeed in school than those whose concept of self includes no sense of responsibility. Furthermore, as adults, these youngsters are more likely to become assets to their community. In most cases, children who are encouraged to take on age-appropriate chores and responsibilities tend to become more self-confident and self-reliant adults.

Keep in mind, however, that there are some people who may *seem* to have high self-esteem yet demonstrate no responsibility to their families or communities. For example, a drug dealer may take pride in being one of the "best" dealers in his community—he has achieved success in a domain in which he aspires to excel and is positively viewed by his significant others. However, despite his *feeling* of high worth, he is morally and socially irresponsible. His view of himself is not realistic, but distorted.

A more cogent example for our purposes is the schoolyard bully. Such a child may brag of his prowess to his friends and, in their eyes, be something of a hero. He may "feel good" about himself, but he is not demonstrating a sense of empathy and personal responsibility.

—Frankie, Age 15—

"I don't get it. I'm still failing. You told me to do all my homework. I did and I even got it in on time. I told ya, the teacher hates me," said Frankie.
"Frankie," I said, "You failed every test. You are responsible to hand in all your homework on time and to study for tests." He looked at me as if he had just heard this for the first time.

Like many other students, especially high school students, he needed to know and understand what his responsibilities as a student were and commit to fulfilling them. Though what these responsibilities are may seem obvious to adults, there are, in fact, youth who have no idea from where their grades come, what they mean, or how to go about improving them. It is a good idea for teachers, perhaps at the beginning of a term, to reiterate in detail for *all* students what they are responsible for and the rationale behind their responsibilities.

I'm sure most of you would agree that a comprehensive list of student responsibilities includes the following:

- The student will be prepared for class by previewing the relevant material the day/night before.
- The student will arrive at the classroom on time.
- The student will be engaged, i.e., participate in the class.
- The student will hand in assignments on time.
- The student will do all assigned homework.
- The student will be organized and motivated to learn.
- The student will study for exams.

Clearly, if all students kept to these standards, we'd have a lot of extremely happy parents and even happier teachers. Unfortunately, however, only a portion of students come anywhere close and even they drop the educational ball once in a while. As with trust, education about personal responsibility must begin in the home, but teachers can reinforce understanding of the role it plays in the academic environment.

Our Responsibilities as Teachers

Like trust, however, to expect students to fulfill their responsibilities requires that we fulfill ours to *them*, as defined by the InTASC standards. Those standards include, but aren't limited to the following.

Treat Students as the Unique Individuals They Are

—Joey, Age 12—

"Joey, is there something wrong?" I asked.

"It's those teachers. I think they're losin' it," he replied.

"What do you mean?"

"Well, they get nuts if you forget a pencil! I'm talkin' about a pencil!" With each word his voice got louder. "I have to remember which room to go to each period, how to get there, what book I need, if I have my homework, if I can get to the bathroom in those few minutes before class and if it's A, B, C, or D day — and they want me to remember a pencil too?"

Joey's teacher hadn't realized how limited he was with respect to remembering things. Children like Joey, who are forgetful and disorganized, have to use all their resources just to survive each day. Unless teachers and other adults understand how difficult it is for such a child, they will not be able to relate to him effectively or provide a measure of respect.

Know Your Subject Matter Well

Incompetence in one's subject matter compromises trust, creates confusion and generates ill will — none of which enhances the learning experience. In the Danielson Framework, it is the very first subdomain of teacher evaluation, and rightly so. Albert Einstein is purported to have said, "If you can't explain it to a six-year-old, you don't understand it well enough yourself." We think it a good rule of thumb for judging your own command of content.

We have seldom, if ever, encountered teachers providing grossly incorrect information. However, we *have* found it relatively common for them to rely heavily on teachers' guides, failing to utilize alternative strategies for delivering content. Similarly, new teachers or those not yet comfortable with new material sometimes miss opportunities for learning by failing to acknowledge equally correct responses simply because the guides don't happen to include them.

At the same time, we are aware that today's teachers are faced with considerable external pressure to conform to externally-imposed standards, including the CCSS and it's admittedly easier, because of time constraints, to accept only those answers the guides provide. Just be careful that reliance on the teacher's guide doesn't become the rule rather than the exception for you, causing you to miss chances to provide genuine success opportunities.

Use a Variety of Learning Tools to Engage Your Students

Present material using a variety of learning tools including, but not limited to books, computers, audio/visual material, maps and globes, charts and graphic organizers. Use the latest technologies available, as well as quality textbooks and other traditional educational resources.

We know from research that when students are involved in multi-faceted, multi-sensory, activity-based lessons, their brains are more fully stimulated and they are more likely to be engaged. This helps not only with motivation to learn and self-esteem, but also provides opportunities for students to develop discipline and acquire needed skills while interacting productively with other students.

Integrate Reading, Writing and Math into All Subjects

We all have a responsibility to reinforce the fact that the proverbial "Three Rs"are valuable tools in addition to being the desired outcome of learning in the early grades. A solid foundation in the fundamentals of communication and calculation serve to facilitate learning in higher level grades. Without skills in reading and comprehension, the lessons of history and literature are largely inaccessible; without math, the ability to perform and interpret scientific data is compromised. No matter what the subject area, include assignments requiring skills in reading, writing and math when you can.

Continue Learning Yourself

We have a responsibility to ourselves as learners, too — to expand our knowledge on the subjects we teach and learn new teaching methodologies, developments or tools that may enhance our effectiveness in the classroom. Take up a new hobby or learn a new skill totally outside of your normal area of expertise. Keep up to date by reading and watching documentaries in your field and in any field that interests you. Consider taking courses, whether local adult education or continuing education courses at local colleges, or more advanced graduate level or professional development courses (local or online). And, of course, don't hesitate to wander outside your normal experience. Teachers need to grow and learn too.

Employ a Variety of Methods for
Evaluating Student Progress

Use a variety of assessments, including oral tests, essays and class presentations to evaluate student mastery. Some students are better at writing, some at speaking, some at hands-on demonstrations of what they've learned. Limiting the modes through which students can show mastery denies some students who may understand the subject matter, especially those who are learning-disabled, adequate opportunity to demonstrate what they've learned and thereby experience success.

Monitor Your Own Progress, Too

If your entire focus is on improving the success of your students, you may overlook an important factor—how well you're doing in delivery. Take time to assess your own progress. Are your students progressing and learning the material to your satisfaction? If not, are there things you do or are not doing that might have a positive impact?

Finally, remember to evaluate individual students independently of each other, but examine class performance as a whole as a strategy for measuring your effectiveness. None of us is perfect—if you see room for improvement, rethink the methods and strategies you use in your classroom. Don't be afraid to try something new and above all, don't be hesitant to share ideas with other teaching professionals. Students need us, but we need each other, too.

Conclusion

The sooner students learn what their responsibilities are, the sooner they begin to experience and take ownership and control over their lives and their performance. With increased control comes opportunity to experience success and accurately attribute that success to one's abilities and effort, thereby enhancing self-esteem. All of this contributes to developing a sense of responsibility, a pillar of good character.

Chapter 8

Options

—Barbara, Age 16—

"My English teacher said that I could do an extra project to get my grade up. I have to because I can't get into a good college with a 'C' in English."

"Why are you running a 'C' in English? Are you missing homework or are you getting low grades on the tests?" I asked.

"Both," said Barbara.

"Why do you miss homework assignments? Is it that you forget about them?"

"Oh, no," said Barbara. "I never forget. I just can't get to them."

"What else are you doing that keeps you from doing the work?" I asked.

"I have all the other homework to do. Then I have lacrosse practice in the spring and fall and basketball in the winter. I also babysit every day and don't get home until after 7:00 p.m.," said Barbara.

At that point, I had Barbara create a chart showing her daily schedule. Between getting up before 6:00 am Monday through Friday, taking all honors and AP courses, going straight to lacrosse practice or basketball practice every day and then babysitting until 6 or 7 p.m., it was no wonder she didn't have the time to complete all her homework assignments.

When I asked what her weekends were like, she revealed that she worked at the local pharmacy and was also taking an SAT prep course. It was clear that not only did she not have time to do an extra project to get her faltering grades up, but that she didn't have time to do anything well. She was overbooked, overtired and overstressed.

I asked her why she was taking only honors and AP courses and she said she wanted to get into a good college. When I asked her why she played lacrosse and basketball, she said that it would look good on her college application. I learned that she babysat and worked at the pharmacy so that she'd have more money to pay for college.

Barbara's ultimate goal was an honorable one—getting into a good college. But she had succumbed to trying to do too much instead of exploring and evaluating options for how to accomplish her goals without wearing herself out. When students take on too much, something invariably suffers. In Barbara's case, it negatively influenced her ability to study and get homework done—and consequently, her grades.

To help Barbara begin to work though solving the problem of her overload, I gave her a chart like the one shown on the next page.

Problem	Option 1	Option 2	Option 3

This is what she came up with:

Problem	Option 1	Option 2	Option 3
1. Overloaded after school	Drop one of the sports activities	Cut back on babysitting	Drop weekend job
2. Courses too demanding	Talk to school counselor	Talk to parents	Talk to teachers to see how much work is required in less demanding courses
3. Not facing reality	Talk to school counselor about a realistic workload	Talk to college admissions counselors about their expectations	Talk to a professional outside of school about the need to accept who you are

Note: While in the example, this chart was used by an individual student, it is equally useful for families and groups of any kind.

Teaching Students to Identify Options

1. What was Barbara's goal? *Getting into a good college.*
2. What was the reality? *She had a C in English, which, as she said, wouldn't help her get into a good college.*
3. What were her options?

The last one is where most children—indeed, most people in general—often need help. The answers, of course, vary according to the individual child and his or her own talents, challenges and circumstances.

Understanding that there are options in life and learning how to first identify and then weigh those options are critical parts of human development and good decision-making. These skills lay the foundation for students to begin to take responsibility for their own behavior, especially as it relates to their performance in school. As students see more clearly the connections between what they do and resultant success or failure in achieving their goals, the more often they choose the options that benefit them most.

However, we see more and more children coming to school—and into our tutoring practice—unaware that options even exist (and frankly some of their parents, too). If you don't know you have options, how skilled can you be in evaluating one vs. another and choosing the one with the highest probability of getting you where you want to be?

Again, just as teachers play an important role in undergirding their students' self-esteem and modeling reciprocal trust relationships, they can assist them in developing the skills that directly impact achievement.

Offering students options whenever feasible in the classroom and providing opportunities for them to explore the results of those choices give children practice in an important step in decision-making and in turn, help lay the groundwork for effective goal-directed behavior, which we will discuss at length in Chapter 10.

Having the opportunity to practice setting goals, identifying and evaluating options based on whether they lead us toward or away from achieving those goals and experiencing success as a result of our efforts all enhance our self-esteem.

Facilitating Decision-Making Skills in the Classroom

The old adage is true. *Practice makes perfect.*

When a situation arises that requires a decision that will affect your students, invite them to participate. Staying within age-appropriate limits, take them through the steps of decision-making. Help them set goals that relate to meeting the objectives of your lesson plans and then involve them in brainstorming options and letting them choose.

By starting small and walking your students through the process of resolving small issues, you'll help them develop skills that apply equally well to the larger, more complex issues that will come their way.

You know your students far better than we, so you're probably way ahead of us in thinking of ways to facilitate the development of your students' decision-making skills. But here are a few ideas for how, in the classroom, you might give them practice in weighing options, which will prepare them to take ownership and responsibility for succeeding in school.

Elementary School Students

Give children opportunities to choose their own treats, provided they are appropriate for the whole class. Allow them to choose from a group of books the ones you will read to them or that they will read to themselves. Talk about decisions they need to make as the seasons change — warm clothes vs. cool clothes, for example. Talk about decisions they need to make about their food choices — junk food vs. healthful food. Discuss the possible ramifications for their choices, e.g., talk about how eating only junk food over a long period of time would make them feel. Use your own creativity — be on the lookout for opportunities in the daily routine to exercise your students' decision-making skills.

Middle School Students

As students get older and more mature, the focus of their decision-making becomes broader. You might discuss the pros and cons of essays vs. multiple-choice exams, or what after-school activities they will choose to participate in — sports, volunteer projects, clubs — and why. They may have choices over classes, e.g., which foreign language course to enroll in. If, in your school's curriculum, students have a choice between French and Spanish, have them explore their options by talking to people who have taken both courses, researching via the internet in what countries these languages are spoken and identifying careers in which fluency in a foreign language is an advantage.

If you're teaching history, revisit major events, like the American Revolution. There are many wonderful historical novels for young readers which detail decisions the colonists had to make. Talk about the pros and cons of going to war.

The book, *My Brother Sam is Dead* by James Lincoln Collier and Christopher Collier, is an ideal book about decision-making for grades five through eight.

High School Students

If you're a high school teacher, *your* challenge is one of narrowing the list of topics for discussion. High school students are faced with a number of choices with respect to academic courses, careers, dating, social situations and colleges.

Older teens start thinking about the skills and talents they have and which career paths might be most suitable for them. As with middle school, assigned books are excellent jumping off points to discuss decision-making. For example, *The Red Badge of Courage* by Stephen Crane allows readers to observe characters as they weigh options and make life and death decisions, in the context of the Civil War.

The Options You Have in Lesson Planning

Every day of our lives, we are faced with the task of choosing between options. Which route will I take to work? Will I ride the bus or drive? Will I eat yogurt and fruit or bacon and eggs?

We narrow those options based on which give us the best opportunity to succeed in attaining our objectives. Which route is more likely to get us to work on time? Which mode of transportation will better allow us extra time to finish a report that is due today? Are we trying to lower our cholesterol or increase our protein intake?

The same is true with respect to instruction. Every time you sit down to plan a lesson, you assess your options. Every day that you walk into your classroom, whether consciously or unconsciously, you will choose to act based on the options you have. Between current theories of learning and advances in technology, the options we have to choose from as teachers are many and varied, by design.

If teaching about Gettysburg, will I lecture from the teacher's guide? Will I bring artifacts or replicas from the Civil War to class and pass them around the room? Will I have my students watch a movie about Lincoln? Will I have them memorize the Gettysburg Address and recite it?

Will I assess student learning with a multiple-choice test having them match the battle and the year? Will I ask them to write an essay comparing and contrasting the basic positions of the Union and the Confederacy? Will I separate them into groups and have them conduct a mock debate?

What must drive your choices is the mission of every teaching professional — to give every student equal opportunity to 1) acquire skills and knowledge through a multisensory approach and 2) understand the material you present through exploration on a variety of cognitive levels.

Let's review what we know about each.

Learning Styles

—Brianna, Age 9—

"I'm learning about density," said Brianna.
"What is density?" I asked.
"Well, you have these little boxes and you color them in different colors," replied Brianna, confidently.
"Why do you color them different colors?" I asked.
"To make the picture pretty. I used red, pink, purple and green," Brianna replied.

Brianna obviously had no idea what "density" meant. Unfortunately, her teacher had no idea she was clueless. Why?

This child needed to concretely "experience" what she was learning—she was a *kinesthetic/tactile* learner. When the teacher explained the definition of density and had Brianna draw pictures to help her understand the concept, no real increase in knowledge occurred. However, when Brianna and I took an empty mayonnaise jar and we incrementally added crayons to "increase the mass while keeping the volume the same," she begin to understand the concept.

Knowing your students' learning styles and choosing options for communicating concepts and terms makes for higher efficiency in learning. As you're reading this book, you're taking in information through all of your senses— you're *seeing* words, *touching* the book or e-reader and *hearing* the sound of the pages as you turn them. At the same time, you may be eating a snack while you read or taking in the smell of a newly-mown lawn from an open window. Chances are that, to acquire new information, you prefer one of your senses over the others. That's only natural — learning is easier for you that way.

Even so, regardless of which sense you use, that acquired information remains as a trace in your brain for only two to four seconds. Yes, you read that right — you'll forget everything in your sensory memory after about four seconds unless it finds its way into your short-term memory.

Since what we see, hear and do needs to be stored first in short-term memory on its way to long-term memory, how it gets there and what is "kept" plays a major role in learning. As a result, it only makes good sense to teach using a *multisensory approach,* which allows every student the opportunity to learn using his or her preferred mode. Because there is no way to know in the beginning of a school year which student uses which learning style with greatest success, this strategy also gives every student an opportunity to succeed from the first day.

The three main learning styles are: **visual, auditory** and **kinesthetic/tactile**.

Visual Learners

If students learn more easily by *seeing* the material, they may be visual learners. Here are some strategies that will help those students:

- Use charts, maps, time lines, or any image or graphic, including graphic organizers, that will help them visualize the information.
- Have them use colored pencils, pens, or markers to write down information. Visual learners often organize by color.

- Have them follow along in the book while you speak and have them physically put "sticky notes" next to the pages you covered in class.
- Have them follow an outline you've prepared.
- Instead of just reading their class notes, suggest that students rewrite sections of their notes when studying.
- When teaching vocabulary, have your students fold a piece of lined paper in half vertically. Have them write four or five vocabulary words on the left side and definitions on the right side. Once they've practiced them, they can rewrite just their words or just the definitions on a second folded sheet to test their knowledge before moving on to a second set of words.
- Show them how to create acronyms (words formed from the first letters of other words) to help retain and recall facts.
- Show them ways to visualize material they need to learn. If they've never tried to use visualization, start by having them visualize the entrance to the school, picturing themselves walking along, seeing the sights, hearing the sounds, breathing the scents, etc. Using a common focal point allows students to share with others the details of their rich visualizations. Building on that, they can move on to create an image in their minds of a character in a story or a famous event in history. This will make what they need to learn much more "real," because they've "seen" it in their mind's eye.
- Have them use the textbook and any other written materials as much as possible.
- Recommend they go online to find images and videos about subjects they're learning. Encourage them to

watch related programs on *PBS* or *The History* or *Smithsonian Channels*. Suggest they rent, or borrow from the library, videos about famous people or events they're studying.

- Encourage them to write whenever possible. This allows them to see the "image" of the words. (Writing can also be helpful for kinesthetic learners.)

Auditory Learners

If students seem to learn more easily by listening to what others say, they may be auditory learners. Here are some strategies that will help those students:

- Keep talking! Present material in a dynamic vocal manner so students really hear what you have to say.
- Show your students how to sub-vocalize, that is, talk to themselves either quietly or silently by moving their lips. This helps students "hear" the information they need to learn.
- Have them make up stories about what they're learning and share them with family members. If no one is available to listen, they can even tell stories to their pets or stuffed animals!
- Have them make up songs and rhymes and then sing the new material to themselves. This can also be used as a fun class activity whether done as solos, duets, or as a class chorus. (This worked well for those of us who learned the alphabet by singing the "ABC Song" and the number of days in each month by repeating the rhyme, "30 days has September, April, June and November...")

Kinesthetic/Tactile Learners

If students seem to learn more easily by writing things down, making tangible models and drawing pictures of what they're learning, they may be kinesthetic/tactile learners. Here are some strategies that will help students who are "hands-on" learners:

- Have them make models to help themselves learn new material and demonstrate their understanding. These could range from building a three-dimensional topographical map to performing simple science experiments.
- Use globes, maps and charts in class and suggest the use of them at home.
- Encourage role-play by having them "act out," alone or in groups, what they're learning.
- Go on field trips. Have your students experience their lessons by visiting museums, historic sites or landmarks.
- Have them write, scribble, doodle and draw pictures related to the topics being taught. The use of their hands in creating pictures helps students "feel" what they're trying to learn.

Take Care Not to Pigeonhole, Though

Though we seem to learn more easily through one sense over another, we still learn through our other senses as well. You may be primarily a visual learner, but you still take things in through your ears, too.

Teaching by using a multi-sensory approach kills two birds with one stone—putting students whose learning styles are different from those of others on an equal footing for learning, while providing a broader base of understanding for all students, irrespective of those styles.

Cognitive Levels

Just you have options for lesson planning based on a range of learning styles among individuals, remember that there's also a range of levels of *thinking* that we use when we learn entirely new material or build on things previously learned. The area of study relating to this concept is often referred to as *depth of knowledge.*

For a long time the educational community has wrestled with how to encourage students to operate using a wider range of cognitive levels. Even more challenging, they've been struggling with how to *evaluate* the extent to which students succeed at operating at these various levels and teachers succeed in planning lessons that utilize those levels. Yet one of the core criteria used in developing the Common Core State Standards was as follows: "Include rigorous content and *application of knowledge through high-order skills...*"

Traditional instruction has historically emphasized recall and understanding with cursory attention to application. This will not suffice in the 21st century. Students need to be challenged by projects and activities that encourage them to do something new and different with what they have learned. That skill, already highly prized in our society, will be essential for future leaders in the global economy.

Before moving on to a discussion of application, let's review the major models relating to cognitive levels and educational objectives based on those models.

Bloom's Taxonomy

One widely-used model was developed in 1956 by Benjamin S. Bloom. Called the "Taxonomy of Educational Objectives," it is often referred to as "Bloom's Taxonomy." This framework has been used by K-12 teachers, as well as college instructors.

Bloom identified six levels of cognitive activity, described them and placed them in a hierarchical order, that is, from simplest behaviors to the most complex. Accordingly, he collectively called the higher three "the invention level." It was a reasonable assumption, based on our knowledge at the time, that learners must normally master the lower levels before being able to advance to the higher levels.

The Bloom learning domains are/were:

1. Knowledge: Recalling information.

2. Comprehension: Understanding the meaning of the information.

3. Application: Using the information by applying it to a novel situation.

4. Analysis: Separating the information into its component parts in order to see how the parts fit into the whole.

5. Synthesis: Combining parts of information to form a new whole, literally to synthesize new meaning from the parts.

6. Evaluation: Judging the value of ideas using objective and comprehensive criteria.

In *A Taxonomy for Learning, Teaching and Assessing (Pearson, 2000)*, this model was modified to increase its relevance in 21st century work. The main revision was that the category names were changed from nouns to *verbs* and the order of the highest two levels was reversed.

As the original model focuses on learning and thinking, this modification addresses and emphasizes measuring results. Arguably, learning and thinking are more important than testing but since student performance, whether dictated by "No Child Left Behind" or "Race to the Top," is difficult to measure quantifiably without test scores, the revised version of Bloom's Taxonomy is more test-friendly. A chart showing the two versions side by side appears below.

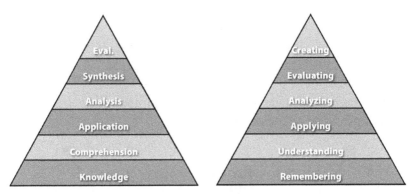

Since then, even newer models have been developed. While they have striking similarities to the revised Bloom model, they seem to be simpler to understand and easier to use for lesson planning and other practical purposes.

These models focus on the "depth of knowledge" students attain for a given subject or topic. Because it's difficult to predict which model(s) will withstand the test of time, we describe below one fairly new model currently in the forefront. But remember, any model that encourages a wide range of thinking in students is a valuable educational tool, so if you have a choice, select one that fits your own conceptualizations and provides you with the most concrete support for evaluating higher level thinking.

Webb's Depth of Knowledge (DOK)

The Depth of Knowledge (DOK) model was first introduced by Norman Webb in 1997. It has four progressive levels, each representing a degree of understanding a student should be able to demonstrate as a result of your instruction.

Level 1. Recall
Level 2. Skill/Concept
Level 3. Strategic Thinking
Level 4. Extended Thinking

Instead of a pyramid, we think the figure below is a more meaningful graphical representation of what happens as depth of knowledge increases.

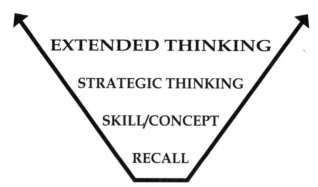

Which level a teacher chooses to use in a given lesson *depends on the objective of the lesson,* the age and grade level of the student, and the nature of the concept itself.

For example, if your goal for students is for them to memorize the state capitals, then the lowest level, recall, is all the student needs to employ.

However, if the objective of the lesson is to understand the causes of the Revolutionary War or contemplate what might have kept the colonists and the British out of war, a higher level of cognition is required.

Since engaging students in lessons that use varying depths of knowledge are among the standards of the InTASC and therefore most teacher evaluation rubrics, if you are observed while teaching a lesson that requires only the lowest levels, address that with your evalutor offline or consider modifying your lesson plans to introduce materials that lend themselves more easily to higher order thinking.

Here are samples from various subjects of how one might implement the DOK model in lesson planning. Once you fully grasp the difference between the levels yourself, I'm sure you'll be even more creative.

If the goal of the lesson is to RECALL:

English: Have your students tell about the story they read by answering the five "W's": who, what, when, where and why.

Math: Have your students write the formulas for finding the area of a triangle, square and rectangle.

Science: Have each student identify and tell the class about a particular element on the periodic table.

Social Studies: Have your students match events in history with the people involved in the particular historical event. Then have them recite a quote from one of those people.

If the goal of the lesson is to have your students learn a new SKILL or understand a new CONCEPT:

English: Ask your students to interpret and summarize a challenging passage from a book they're reading.

Math: Ask your students to use context cues to determine what they need to do to solve a math problem.

Science: Ask your students to predict what will happen if they hold their breath for as long as they can.

Social Studies: Show a video of the Lewis and Clark expedition. Then have your students pretend they're reporters and summarize the events that occurred as Lewis and Clark traveled.

If the goal of the lesson is to have your students THINK STRATEGICALLY:

English: After reading two short stories, ask your students to compare the main characters of each story by citing evidence to show who was a stronger character and why.

Mathematics: Ask your students to develop a logical argument as to why a fence builder would only be concerned about the perimeter of a property and not about the area while the opposite would be true for a house painter.

Science: Have your students use concepts they've learned previously to calculate how much water must be put into a test tube so it can produce a given musical note when they blow across the top of the tube. (Depending on the grade level, the teacher may have to supply additional information.)

Social Studies: Have your students construct a model of a lock of the Erie Canal.

If the goal of the lesson is to have your students EXTEND their thinking:

English: After reading a book as a class, have your students create a chart putting together all the major turning points in the story.

Math: Analyze and critique the two systems of measurement in use today. Based on your findings, prepare a "pros and cons" argument whether to continue to use both or to adopt only one system.

Science: Ask your students to design and conduct an experiment in which they determine the advantages and disadvantages of using a LED or CF light instead of an incandescent light bulb.

Social Studies: As a class, select a Supreme Court case from at least 50 years ago. Have your students analyze and predict, based on present-day laws, whether the verdict would be the same if the case were tried today. (Remind them to be sure the answers are based on *facts* and not *opinions* they have heard or read.

First Things First

Not all lessons or subject areas lend themselves to involvement at each level of understanding and while not all students will benefit from examination on each level, the need to encourage our students to think at all cognitive levels of cognition is a "no brainer" whose time has finally come.

Having said that, however, there is a method to the madness. Especially in the early grades, the ability to recall basic facts and use them in reading and arithmetic is the primary goal. But recall is not an end in itself. It's the necessary first rung of the ladder. Unless we already know how to add, subtract, multiply and divide, trying to solve an algebraic equation is impossible.

Likewise with the act of thinking itself. Unfortunately, in a hurry to implement the CCSS goals of applied thinking, some teachers tend to get ahead of themselves and end up causing confusion and frustration. As with the example above, you can't think at a higher level if you don't understand the vocabulary.

One of the first things we do in our assessment and tutoring practice is determine—before we give an assignment—if a student has all the foundational skills and knowledge he needs to successfully carry out an assignment. What level they "should" be on or what they "should" know is beside the point. If they don't, your only option in an environment conducive to learning is to "meet" the student at the depth of knowledge he or she has and begin from there.

As each student has the opportunity to practice, with your instruction, going through each step to think on higher and higher levels, he will begin to do it himself. Without your guidance, he won't.

Over the years, more and more students have appeared in our tutoring practice not knowing how to study. We see this as a direct result of their not being taken through the steps to higher order thinking in the classroom, much less at home.

On the facing page is a handout from our book *Improve Your Reading Skills,* which we developed to assist our students in improving their reading comprehension skills. It highlights what we call the "TEACH" method. It can be adapted equally well to virtually any subject area.

T–E–A–C–H Method: Overview

T-E-A-C-H is a five-step method by which you teach yourself how to improve your reading comprehension. Each letter in the word **TEACH** stands for a step in the process.

T = Think E = Explain A = Ask C = Clues H = Handwrite

Think

Think about whether or not you will like the assigned reading. Think about whether or not you feel like reading it. If not, then think about where you want to be, what job you want to have, and what kind of person you want to be in the future. Do you need to read this assignment to do well in this course, so that you can have the kind of future you want? If the answer is yes, then you need to face the facts and read the assignment.

Explain

Explain to yourself what you are about to read and, if possible, how it fits or doesn't fit into your life. It makes it easier if you can relate it to something you already know about, something in your memory.

Ask

Ask yourself the **5 W's, 1. Who** do you think are the important characters? 2. **When** do you think the event takes place? 3. **Where** do you think it occurs? 4. **What** do you think it is about? 5. **Why** do you think it takes place?

Clues

You can find clues about what you are about to read, what to focus on when you read, and what's important to remember in your reading, in all sections of books: summary, review, end-of-chapter questions, key words, headings, diagrams & captions, graphs, maps, back cover, and pictures.

Handwrite

Now read. As you read, handwrite the highlights. That is, handwrite everything you read that you think is important. Organize the reading material into an outline, picture-story, or any other graphic organizer. By writing and drawing while you read, you will understand and remember much more.

"Now you're messin' with my head! Am I reading or am I writing?"

– from *Improve Your Reading Skills,* © Strong Learning, Inc.
    www.stronglearning.com

Chapter 9

Needs

— Anthony, Age 16 —

"I don't know why I keep getting such bad grades," said Anthony. "I study every night until 1:00 AM."

Anthony was feeling pretty poorly about himself. He felt there was something wrong with him. No matter how much he studied, he still got C's.

After completing a week's schedule to see how much time he spent actually studying, we discovered that the problem wasn't the amount of time he studied — the problem was his physical condition. He didn't have the energy to study.

He was on the lacrosse team, which had lengthy practice sessions every day after school. He then went to work at the supermarket, because he wanted money to pay for his car. He never ate breakfast because he slept too late, so he would grab a candy bar or doughnut on his way to school.

It's a well-demonstrated fact that a child's basic physical and emotional needs must be met before he can hope to fulfill his potential in school. Yet, there are untold numbers of children sitting in classrooms today who are hungry. There are students—both rich and poor—who are sleep-deprived. There are homeless students and kids who come from wealthy homes who feel physically or emotionally vulnerable. Even in the best of physical conditions, the need to belong, the need to feel respected and the need to feel worthy must be met before a child can effectively learn to read, do math, or write a well-thought-out paper. If you're hungry or anxious, is learning on your mind?

Unfortunately, as teachers, we have very little control over whether our students' basic needs are met, yet in spite of that, our job is to try to teach our students what they need to know to thrive. What can we do? Following are some ideas and examples of what other teachers have done successfully.

The Need to Eat Well

There is no escaping the fact that all humans, especially children and teenagers, need balanced diets with all food groups represented. We know that the quality of children's diets affects the development of their brains and consequently, their likelihood of performing well in school.

We understand, also, that getting kids to eat well is often difficult. Younger children are sometimes picky eaters, while teenagers are often overly concerned with their weight or appearance for social reasons or complain that they're simply too busy to eat properly.

As it was with Anthony, skipping breakfast is among the most common nutritional issues for teenagers. With working parents who are often stressed themselves, school mornings can be such whirlwinds that many kids end up rushing out of their homes without eating anything at all.

But there are many creative solutions that don't require cooking. One which often seems to work well, both in terms of time and nutritional value, is a glass of milk and a single portion of not-too-sweet cereal. It takes almost no time for a child to down the milk and the cereal in a pack can be eaten en route to school.

A math teacher noticed that, despite other efforts, a group of his 9th grade students, who came to him mid-morning, often struggled to remain alert and engaged. He mentioned the breakfast idea to the kids and was pleasantly surprised when, the next day, virtually the whole class bounced into the room, many eagerly sharing that they had eaten breakfast that morning. Their more animated participation in class revealed that they felt a lot better for it. Newly energized, they kept it up for the rest of the year.

What other things can teachers do to increase the likelihood that their students eat well? Though you obviously can't manage your students' lives at home, there are still a few things you can try. For instance:

- If you think a child is not doing well because of missing breakfast or other nutrition issues, talk to the school nurse. She may contact the parents and see what is happening. In the current economy, many schools serve breakfast.
- Even if you're not teaching science or health, take time to talk about how a healthy and alert brain increases the likelihood that kids succeed in school. This is the perfect time to mention how food nourishes the brain.
- Include a lesson in your subject matter that highlights the different food groups. In math, for example, use food to teach percentages or conversions from grams and milligrams to ounces and pounds. Weave simple

facts about food into the discussion if you can. It's a great opportunity to talk about calories, too.

The Need for Adequate Sleep

Sleep deprivation, while an issue for children of any age, is particularly prevalent in teenagers. The average teen needs over nine hours of sleep each night. Younger children need even more. Think about how you feel when you don't get enough sleep and you'll know that it can make teens cranky and blue, ruin their concentration, delay their response times and affect their health long-term.

It's not enough to say to them, "Get to sleep earlier," however. Some scientific studies tell us that teens can't go to sleep too early—their biological clocks won't let them. But you can still influence your students. Talk to them about the importance of sleep. Assist them in identifying and evaluating options for doing so, e.g., doing their homework earlier in the evening (so they get to bed sooner) or sleeping in on weekends so they can catch up on sleep.

Talk with school advocacy groups about the benefits of starting school later in the morning. Do the math—asking our teens to wake up at 5:30 a.m. to catch a school bus at 6:30 a.m. is unproductive at best, especially when most of them go to sleep after 11:00 p.m. At an average of three hours of sleep lost per day, consider the long-term effects. (Yeah, we know, this may get you nowhere, but nothing will happen if we don't at least try.)

As for younger students, if you see a child yawning all day in class or regularly putting her head down on the desk to rest, contact her parents and tell them what's happening. Sometimes a solution as simple as changing bedtime can reap major benefits for a child.

The Need for Adequate Physical Activity

Do you exercise before or after a day of teaching? If so, you're aware of how physical activity can boost your energy in the morning or alleviate stress at the end of your day. Like you, your students need to be physically active, too. Along with proper nutrition and plenty of rest, the health benefits from regular physical activity are numerous. Exercise promotes a sense of wellbeing, reduces the risk for serious health problems such as high blood pressure and diabetes, helps build and maintain healthy bones, muscles and joints, mitigates weight gain and is a great stress-buster. If we stimulate our bodies, we stimulate our brains, improving our abilities to focus and remember, both of which are essential to learning.

Recommendations:

- Give your students physical breaks. Physical activity involves movement, so active play can be good. For elementary students who sit in the same room all day, do jumping jacks or run in place with your class in the middle of the morning. Middle and high school students already move about from one class to another.
- Ensure participation in recess. As we said in the chapter on Trust, for elementary school children, recess is a *must*. When I hear that a child was made to sit in his classroom and complete his morning work rather than join the other kids at recess, I am concerned. As a general rule, the student who doesn't complete his homework or class work may need recess even more than others.

- Encourage enrollment in gym class if it's available. Physical education classes are now mandatory in many school districts and all children should be encouraged to participate.
- Prepare lessons that involve movement. Be creative – this helps young brains (and many older ones as well) process and synthesize new information.

The Need to Manage Stress Effectively

An alarming number of children today experience stress-related problems that in turn hamper their school success. They don't have as much time for play. They have a greater quantity of homework than in the recent past. And sadly, their homes may not be calm, safe places. As it does with adults, prolonged stress negatively affects motivation and concentration, interrupting regular study routines, affecting REM sleep and interfering with academic success.

Like physical exercise, some stress helps to keep our nervous systems in tune. It's the extent and nature of the stressors that determine how much a child will be affected. A 14-year-old once complained to me, "My mother died and my father is about to marry someone I hate. How am I supposed to do school?"

As discussed before, as a teacher, you are one of your students' most important significant others and in a prime position to see what's going on with them. Although you are not likely a trained psychologist or social worker, learn to look for symptoms of debilitating stress in your students and seek professional advice on how you or someone you can recommend might help those students.

And remember that you are not immune to the effects of

stress, either. If your own stress level gets too high, don't be embarrassed to seek professional assistance. Even counselors and physicians seek professional help when they encounter significant pressures outside their control.

Make time for fun in the classroom, too. The lives of some children today are not just stressful, but largely *joyless* as well. Having too many activities and responsibilities to balance — before they've had time to develop the skills to manage them — robs children of the unencumbered fun that is an ideal part of a healthy childhood. It's been demonstrated over and over again — children learn more when they are happy and having fun.

Here are some ideas for incorporating more fun in your classroom.

- Share funny stories about personal experiences, yours and theirs, from the past. Help kids learn to laugh at themselves.
- Go on age-appropriate field trips that the class will enjoy. Include some where kids will be able to be themselves.
- Attend movies, plays, or school functions with your class.
- Go to local school sporting events with your class or even with your own family. Kids love seeing their teachers outside of the classroom.
- Make homework a game with rewards in addition to grades. Near the end of a semester, college professors I know have a game-show type of competition between their chemistry classes. The students report that they study more for the game than they would for their final exams. Healthy competition is an effective motivator and can provide much opportunity for joy and laughter.

- Involve your students as much as possible as active participants in their lessons. For example, a physics teacher had his classes each year use their formulas to calculate how to play different songs using test tubes filled with different levels of water. The songs were played over the school's intercom and the whole school voted on which class's song was best.

It's up to you to establish the climate in your room. Make it a fun place to be and you'll find that your students more easily learn when they don't *know* they're learning. Best of all, you'll probably have a lot of fun, too.

The Need for Safety

Considering how much of children's formative years are spent there, the school environment should be one of safety and security. It is difficult for students to develop positive self-images and concentrate in school if their days are spent in fear or emotional neglect. If children live in areas that are not safe or if they are terrorized by bullies, gangs and other delinquents, they will not usually function well in school.

Safety issues weigh heavily on children. A proactive approach to mediation of real threats is desirable. While you have no control over their home environments, you do have influence over your classroom. School can and should be a safe haven for kids and you can help mitigate the effects of external concerns or fears by ensuring that your students perceive that school is a positive and nurturing place to be because it *is*.

Most schools today have security measures in place with teachers or monitors always on the lookout to remedy situations that cause some students to feel unsafe. However, because some issues sneak "under the radar" or cannot be avoided, keep alert for little signs. Be vigilant with respect to signals that the physical or emotional safety of a child is threatened — sudden changes in behavior and deteriorations in school performance are good indicators. These include lack of concentration (daydreaming), acting out, declining grades, or in more severe cases, shutting down emotionally.

In the wake of tragedies like Newtown, even the most self-confident of kids exhibit these behaviors. It is human nature to focus on safety issues when widely-known incidents occur, but there are many children who felt or were unsafe long before Newtown and there will be some who will feel unsafe when the last vestiges of sensationalism have passed. No matter what or when, the need for children to feel safe, physically and emotionally, in the classroom must be fulfilled if we expect them to perform at a maximum level in school.

As we discussed in the chapter on Trust, it is important that we convey to students that *we are their allies* and are working toward the same goals. When there is a problem, students need to feel comfortable coming to us for help or guidance even when the issues are peripheral to the classroom.

Safety issues at school are basically the same as those at home — students need to feel safe from physical, verbal, emotional and social abuse. A major difference between home and school is that in school, there are many more opportunities to be ridiculed, humiliated, made fun of, picked on, physically abused, or punished. In the first place, at school, there are hundreds of children, many of whom are bent on building themselves up at the expense of others. In addition, there are unfortunately a number of adults who are either uninformed about or insensitive to the needs of children. There are clearly still others who exploit them, especially those most vulnerable.

While there are safety "checks and balances" in place in most schools, there are occasional cracks—even gaping holes—where children sometimes feel unsafe despite the best intentions of the adults who run schools and classes. Playgrounds, lunchrooms, bathrooms, school buses and bus stops, to name a few, have proven, on occasion, to have "unsafe" written all over them. Needless to say, this takes a toll on academic performance.

If you suspect anything is happening at school that could be a threat to student safety, immediately raise the issue with other teachers or school administrators. Keep an eye out for students who may be potential troublemakers as well as for those who may be vulnerable.

When an opportunity presents itself, assure your students that they are safe at school and that school personnel will protect them. If appropriate, point out how officials have worked with parents to create an effective emergency plan. Provide as much information as students and their parents require in order to be reassured that school is a safe place. Encourage school officials to conduct regular disaster drills just as they do with fire drills. (While many children overtly dismiss these as silly, most find them to be a source of comfort, especially with some of the severe weather conditions or natural disasters they hear about on the news.) Knowing their teachers and school administrators have a plan helps them kids feel safer and better able to focus on their studies.

While controversial, consider allowing students to have cell phones with the contingency that they may only be used with your permission. Many children enjoy the luxury of carrying their own cell phones—just knowing that they can make contact with their parents in an emergency makes them feel safer. Though some schools ban cell phone use for good reason, school personnel, police and fire departments can work together to devise reasonable policies regarding their use in emergency situations.

The Need to Play

Fred Rogers once said, "Play is often talked about as if it were a relief from serious learning. But for children play is serious learning. Play is really the work of childhood."

Children need to play because it offers opportunities for learning and growth. When children play, they create scenarios from scratch and solve problems. They experience self-sufficiency from playing alone and collaboration through playing with others. When a group of nine and ten-year-olds decide to play tag in the schoolyard, they have the opportunity to make, change and obey rules. They also learn how to strategize and to cooperate. Most importantly, they have fun. In your classroom, provide opportunities for elementary school children to play with blocks, clay, scraps of wood or fabric, weights, magnets, paper clips and even food. These children will be learning while they create. They'll have to read directions and recipes, measure, count, write and cooperate and a host of wonderful things we can't anticipate.

Make time for middle and high school students to participate in science fairs, cooking, debates, school plays and other hands-on activities. Learning by playing familiar games with special cards can be fun. With the appropriate material, games like "Jeopardy," "Go to the Head of the Class," "Bingo," "Lotto," "Concentration," and "Go Fish" also engage teenagers.

Your Needs Count, Too:
Help For the Overworked Teacher

Teaching can be an exhausting profession. You're on stage all day and you work hard. When you get home, you're undoubtedly tired, but often have papers or tests to grade and lessons to prepare for the next day.

Your needs are the same as your students. When in the classroom, their needs always come first, but treat yourself well when you're not on stage. Make sure that you:

Exercise.

Be sure there's time in your schedule to exercise. This will help you maintain your health and reverse the effects of stress built up during the school day. Some teachers work out in their school gyms, others walk or run during lunch. Still others are members of health clubs or attend exercise or dance classes.

Eat well.

As one teacher once told me, "When I get home, I could eat the refrigerator." When we're tired, it's easy to opt for fast food over cooking or snack on whatever's available.

As children, some of us came home to find milk and cookies waiting, so it's easy to grab that bag of Oreos in the pantry, but if you're like me, your metabolism isn't what it used to be. Take time to prepare nutritious snacks for yourself.

Get enough rest.

Just like students, many adults, especially teachers, are sleep-deprived. The average adult needs six to eight hours of sleep per night—even more as we get older. But, between correcting papers, running errands, helping your own kids with their homework, or getting up in the night with babies and young children, teachers are often as exhausted as their students.

It's a given that kids get sick sometimes, so if you have young children, plan ahead—consider what you can change or cut out of your schedule so that you get more sleep. If you're a single parent and can afford it, hire a "mother's helper" after school so you can take a nap. If your spouse is willing and available, have him (or her) take charge of helping with homework or doing more of the daily household chores. If you can, meditate for 10-20 minutes in the morning or evening. Even a little goes a long way.

Conclusion

Creating a classroom environment conducive to learning is not possible when children's basic human needs aren't met. Students and teachers need nutritious food, sufficient sleep and physical exercise to keep their bodies and brains in good working order. Physical and emotional safety, including protection from both real and perceived threats, skills and strategies for managing stress and opportunities to play and rest are essential to emotional wellbeing. When any of these needs goes unfulfilled, academic performance eventually suffers.

Your success as a teacher depends as much on whether your students are physically and emotionally prepared to learn as on your own knowledge of subject matter or teaching style. You can't control most of the circumstances that contribute to deficiencies in your students' physical and emotional health, but you can learn to recognize the associated symptoms, do what you can to mitigate the circumstances and remain alert to situations that may interfere with your students' perception that your classroom is a safe, and consequently, fun place to learn.

Chapter 10

Goals

"I really want to do good in school. I study and everything!"exclaimed Will.

"When do you study?" I asked. "For example, how much time do you put aside to do your homework and study for tests on Mondays?"

"Oh, I guess before I go to bed, around 11:00 p.m."

"Why do you wait until then?" I asked.

"Well, after school I have football. Then I come home and eat dinner, take a shower and then I go on Facebook."

I asked Will what he did the other nights of the week, after he got home from school or football. His answer revealed that between showering, eating dinner and engaging with friends via social media, there was little time left for homework and studying.

Will was motivated to do well and appeared to be organized, but didn't realize that he was, in effect, choosing to fail by spending his free time doing everything other than studying, or that the choices he was making were taking a toll on his grades.

But, unlike Barbara in Chapter 8, Will's issue was not one of not knowing he had options, making poor choices or trying to do too much, but of being unaware of the *connections* between his choices and achieving goals.

The prefrontal cortex — the part of the brain that deals with executive functions like decision-making — develops during the teenage years. For some that happens earlier than for others. Consequently, adults often need to intervene to help teens begin to make decisions and take responsibility for their behavior (and its outcome), which is integral to the lifestyle of the successfully functioning student.

In order to introduce to Will the importance of goals, I asked him what career he was interested in pursuing. His knee-jerk reaction was classic. "What?" and then, "I don't know."

I followed by asking if he wanted to go to college.

"Of course," he replied.

It was obvious from our conversation that, as hard to believe as it may sound, Will didn't see the connection between grades and acceptance into college.

I pulled from my shelf a huge book of four-year colleges and we proceeded to pick out a few he thought he might be interested in attending. We looked up each college's GPA requirements for admission, compared them to his then-current grade point average and calculated what grades he'd need to earn in order to raise his GPA to a level where most of the colleges he wanted to attend would even consider him for admission.

Fortunately, it was mathematically possible.

We started by setting some short-term goals — goals that could be achieved within a few short days — and before long, Will began to see that the goal we had set together — that of raising his GPA — was attainable. After that, with some help, he was able to add increasingly longer-range goals to the plan.

Establishing Goals

Goals provide children and adults alike with destinations—targets to reach for. As such, they give us direction and purpose. But as with our discussion on options in Chapter 8, unless introduced to the concept of setting them, kids don't magically get the connections between what they want in the future and what they do now.

Research has shown that children who learn how to establish and attain realistic short- and long-term goals—based on social standards compatible with their own talents, desires and needs—reach higher levels of success than those who don't. As their adults and mentors, it is up to us to help them set and evaluate realistic school-related goals and to find the means that will enable them to attain those goals. This also involves helping them learn to identify and weigh options and develop strategies for confronting and overcoming obstacles in their paths, which we'll tackle in Part III.

Though the ability to acquire the full complement of decision-making skills doesn't fully develop until the teenage years, it's never too early to begin to establish goals. Even elementary school children benefit from learning to create and attain goals, no matter how modest.

The two types of goals we've been discussing should be presented to students when appropriate. They are:

1. **Short-term goals.** For today, next week, or the near future, they are often simple, but not necessarily easy to attain.
2. **Long-term goals.** Like targets for the future, they are often less tangibly defined than short-term goals and require more steps and more complex actions to attain.

Some short-term goals are first steps towards attaining long-term goals. For example, a child who aspires to play professional baseball (long-term goal) has to first learn how to bat and throw well (short-term goals).

Many of the high-school kids who come to my office have impressive long-term goals. They talk about applying to top colleges and eventually becoming CEOs, doctors, or lawyers. Yet, like Will, they cut classes, neglect handing in lab work and homework and fail to study adequately for their tests. Clearly, these children need to learn how to identify and evaluate their options and set short term goals that will help them direct their actions toward achieving their stated long-term goals.

When working with your students, begin by focusing on important short-term goals. Show how each task fits into the bigger scheme (for example, passing tests contributes to a good education, which leads to a good career, which leads to a happy life). By helping a child accomplish one homework assignment (an easy-to-explain short-term goal), then another, then a lab report, then another, etc., a child can begin to see that school tasks are not only "do-able" but are also necessary steps to bigger and better things.

Long-term goals, on the other hand, are often meaning-less to students—especially children and young teens. They haven't yet lived long enough to experience success in achieving goals that may be years away. The concept of long-term goals is too vague and too distant to be relevant in the context of their daily lives.

To many children and to some adults as well, the very thought of setting long-term goals is anxiety-producing. The idea of building a career, supporting a future family, buying a house, having and raising children, paying for their children's college education is overwhelming.

The easiest way to reduce that anxiety is by breaking long-term goals down into a series of manageable short-term steps.

Helping Your Students Establish and Meet Short-Term Goals

The first step to achieving any goal, once it is set, is evaluating it. In the workplace, a current focus is that of setting some variation of what are called S.M.A.R.T. goals, goals that are Specific, Measureable, Attainable, Relevant and Timely. (Use this acronym or adjust the language of goal-setting to the grade-level and vocabulary of your students.)

Is the target clearly understood? Is the child capable of achieving it? Can it be accomplished in the time planned? Should the goal be broken down into further steps in order to give your students opportunities to quickly meet them and experience success? How can progress toward the goal be measured and monitored?

Whenever possible, give your students positive and constructive feedback regarding their progress toward achieving their goals. For example, if your student is trying to master the multiplication tables, the parts of the digestive system, or a foreign language, encourage him with statements that remind him of the need for persistence and provide feedback about his progress: "I've noticed how you've stuck with memorizing this," or "You're getting better and better at this every day."

- Especially with younger children, **use tangible, easy-to-understand reward systems to provide feedback.** Giving elementary school children stars or stickers when they achieve a significant goal makes them feel proud, not only because they receive recognition, but because they provide visible feedback that they have accomplished a goal. No matter how old they are, kids feel valued when adults acknowledge and reward their achievements.

- **Help your students identify and avoid or overcome potential obstacles to achieving their goals.** For example, a student who wants to score 100 on a test may have to postpone a social activity to make time to study and to avoid going to bed too late the night before. A "refresher" on choosing options based on what the expected result will be may be in order.

- **Be consistent and genuine with encouragement.** If a child is struggling, seek to neutralize frustration and reinforce persistence by recounting her successes in previously performed tasks. Remind her, for example, that she has gotten A's before and to think about how she prepared for that test or project, or what she did to get the grade she aspired to. Since it's hard to talk to each student privately, you can discuss past achievements as a group, taking care not to focus on any one student. Have students write about their success experiences and then share with the class what they did to achieve a good grade on a test or a paper they wrote, a math problem they figured out, or even a non-school-related task, like getting dinner on the table for their family.

- **At intervals, re-evaluate goals and obstacles.** If your students struggle to attain short-term goals, reevaluate the goals and obstacles and explore ways to revise or simplify them so as to increase the number of success experiences they have.

Helping Your Students Establish and Meet Long-Term Goals

To facilitate the development of long-term goals, especially with older students, focus on goals they might want to achieve during the school year. This is best done at the beginning of the school year so achievement of short-term goals reinforces persistence, but is logically seen as a benchmark of progress toward long-term goals.

- Have your students think about and write down some objectives they wish to accomplish. These can vary from getting A's on their report cards to making the football team to winning first prize at the science fair or making the honor roll. Once they have written down their thoughts, discuss with them the short-term goals they must set and meet to achieve these goals. For young children, suggest simple goals like making new friends, doing well in school, or acting in a school play.
- Encourage each student to monitor for themselves how they're doing with setting and starting to meet long-term goals. To facilitate this, have your students write down one long-term goal. Then have them write down, in order, the steps they will take to meet that goal. Finally, have them put a deadline beside each step — the date when they expect to have completed the step. At the end of the process, they will have an actionable plan for meeting the goal and the "mile markers" they need to keep an eye on where they are on the journey to attaining it.

Once school goals are set, guide older students to think more about their futures beyond school. Have them visualize what they want to do during their lives, what they want to be when they are adults. Advise them that certain professions require mastery of certain subject areas (doctors need to study biology, oil explorers need to study geology, etc.) so they can see how school connects to work.

The most common reason given by high-school dropouts is that they don't see what schoolwork has to do with "real" life. It follows that perhaps the most fruitful application of long-term goal setting for high school students, is in beginning to explore career paths and think about individuals whose lives they aspire to emulate. As the alignment of educational outcomes with the demands of the future workplace is one of the stated primary objectives of the Common Core State Standards, it's never too early to start the process.

Following are some ideas for using career exploration as a means for teaching students the process of establishing and meeting long-term goals.

Exploring Career Aspirations and Finding Positive Role Models

Help your students visualize what being successful would "look like." A first step is to have them choose a person or persons they admire and describe the qualities those people have that they would like to emulate. Be a role model for your students and to help them find other role models. For example:

- **Ask your students: "When you grow up, what kind of person would you like to be?"** Some may answer that they want to be like you! (If so, either they're putting you on or you're clearly leading by example.) If the answers include some violent archvillain of a comic superhero, don't despair. Students may need more potential role models from which to choose. You, along with the parents, can expose students to new role models firsthand though history, current events, or pop culture.
- **Introduce the many possible careers that are available.** Look for opportunities to discuss careers your students may want to consider or avoid. Have them talk about careers with various people they encounter at school, at home, or in everyday life — some may respect and admire the school athletic coach while others may be interested in what teachers do. Students may get ideas for career-planning when an electrician comes to work at the house, when visiting the doctor or the dentist, or when watching an anchorperson on the evening news. In many cases, it may be possible to talk to one of these professionals about the type of work he does, what skills were needed to get to this position and the lifestyle he leads. That allows students to observe certain traits required in those careers that either match their personality and interests or don't. For example, when a nocturnal kid sees that bakers get up at 3:00 in the morning, that goal would probably be kaput!
- **Talk about famous people.** Well-known historical figures and what they have provided for humankind are good topics for conversation.

When teaching English, history and science, find time to discuss the accomplishments of particular scientists, inventors, explorers, authors, entertainers and sports figures. Your students' imaginations may be aroused and career goals may be inspired.

- **Find people in the community who provide valuable services.** Discuss the roles of firefighters, police officers, storeowners, teachers, doctors, electricians, plumbers and so on. Your students may know people in these roles — talk about who they are and what they do. Or better yet, encourage your students to approach even community figures they don't know and ask them about what they do firsthand. Most would be thrilled to share their experiences.

- **Encourage students to talk to family members and friends who have attributes that are requisite for the work they do.** For example, it may be that the reason Uncle Philip chose to become a firefighter is that he is big and strong. Joanne, a family friend, is caring, kind and a good organizer — maybe that's why she runs the women's shelter. Cousin John knows the city inside and out — that's one of the reasons he's a top notch assignment editor for the TV station.

- **Expose your students to theater, art, music, sporting events, movies, lectures, museums and other stimulating experiences.** Through exposure to the world beyond the family and classroom settings, children are provided with even more role models to emulate, such as athletes, actors, artists, doctors and scientists.

- **Provide access to career resources.** Many libraries and school guidance offices have resources devoted to career opportunities. Encourage your students to visit these resources or invite a guidance counselor to speak to your class. In addition, there are career "theme parks" in various parts of the country that provide full immersion role-playing opportunities for children in various career fields. And, of course, don't forget the internet!

In a sense, goals are like rudders on ships. Realistic short- and long-term goals help us to steer our lives. As a teacher, help your students become good navigators.

Everyone Isn't Good at Everything— We All Succeed at Different Things

The only time in life that we're tested on *everything* is in school. Once out of school, we can follow our abilities and interests to find the job or career that's the right one for each of us and avoid areas we're not so good at.

Some people are born mathematicians and others can't seem to pass math no matter how organized and motivated they are. Some people can't write well, but can tell a great story. Some very quiet students, the ones who hate to speak up in class, can write outstanding essays.

We're all different. That's good news! We need people with diverse aptitudes and interests to keep society healthy and vibrant. Let your students know that they need not be hard on themselves when they can't hit a homerun during physical education class, can't draw well in art class, or can't remember who won what war.

Even if your students realize they're not going to become the next Nobel-prize-winning brain surgeons, encourage them to do whatever it takes to get the best score they can in the classes that give them trouble and then move on to ace the subject(s) in which they excel.

The Goal for Teachers

On many levels, to discuss goal-setting for teachers is redundant here because teaching professionals should have only one overarching goal.

And what is it? That's right—to create classroom environments conducive to learning.

The InTASC standards break that goal into 10 intermediate goals and teacher evaluation systems like that of The Danielson Group have divided them into more measureable goals, if you will.

If you know where you're going, you're more likely to get there, so in the Appendix, we have included summary information about the InTASC Standards, the Danielson Framework, and how practicing the STRONG approach can help you improve your "grades" the next time you are evaluated.

**Goals are like rudders on ships—
they help us to steer our lives.
As a teacher, help your students
become good navigators.**

Conclusion - Part II

The first principle of the STRONG Learning Model relates to self-esteem. That's not an accident. In fact, in the broadest sense, teachers who are most effective in creating environments conducive to learning are those who encourage the development and maintenance of genuinely high self-esteem in their students.

Research has shown that we learn, as children, to hold ourselves in high esteem based on how our significant others, namely our parents and teachers, treat us. If they treat us with respect, we learn to treat ourselves with respect. If they are trustworthy, we emulate them and are trustworthy too.

Research has also shown that a major contributor to self-esteem is confidence in our ability to succeed in situations that are important to us. Second only to the family, school is ideally a protected place where we have the opportunity not only to acquire knowledge in the form of facts and information we will need, but one where we have the opportunity to develop self-confidence and acquire broad skills we will use over and over again throughout our lives. How confident we are in our ability to succeed has everything to do with how we approach goals and tasks and how successful we will be in achieving those goals and performing those tasks. What better way could there be than to apply them in school!

What most determines whether you tackle learning something new? Higher pay for another degree is important, but greater even than that is *your belief that you will succeed.* And why do you have that belief? Because you've experienced successes in the past. The more successes we experience, the more realistic our senses of our abilities (and limitations) and the higher and more stable our self-esteem. If we succeed, the likelihood that we will succeed again increases. In all of life, there is no greater motivation to succeed than the desire to repeat the heady experience of success itself.

In a nutshell, *the environment that is most conducive to learning is one in which there is ample opportunity for every student to experience success.* Knowing your students and knowing them well is key to your ability to providing genuine opportunities for them to succeed.

There are some students who experience success in school no matter what. They don't require a lot from us as teachers. For others, we have to invest more time and energy to identify their learning styles, teach to those styles with lessons involving all the senses and levels of thinking, and work with them to ensure that they experience success in school—no matter how small and insignificant their early successes may seem.

Yes, teachers face many challenges in the 21st century classroom that are largely outside our control, but the "buck" stops with us when it comes to the emotional climates in our classrooms.

We are faced, too, with the effects of hunger, homelessness, sleep deprivation and issues of physical and emotional safety at home and on the school campus. Common sense tells us that if a student is hungry or sleepy or anxious—legitimately or otherwise—his motivation to learn multiplication tables or the causes of the Civil War is diminished, no matter how wonderful our lesson plans. Though we have little influence over the experiences of our students outside the classroom, it is to our benefit to do whatever we can so they are better able to take advantage of opportunities to learn and thereby succeed in changing their own lives.

How successful will we be in preparing the children in our classrooms for the challenges of tomorrow? The answer depends on how STRONG they are.

PART III

The Student

Chapter 11

When Something's Still Wrong

An 8-year-old sits in his desk, doing nothing. All other students in the classroom have picked up their pencils and begun working on the assignment. This isn't the first time it's happened and twice he has failed to turn in his homework. Which of the following is true?

A. He hates me.
B. He should have been kept back.
C. We've tried to help. He's just not interested.
D. His parents are obviously not doing their job.
E. I don't know what is wrong, but he isn't learning, so it's my job to discover what's wrong and do what I can about it.

You've taken care in lesson planning to ensure that you've included activities for children of different learning styles. When the subject matter lends itself to it, you start with recall and build from there to assignments requiring extended thinking.

When they are in your classroom, children feel safe, energetic and engaged. They want to gain your approval because you have proven to be trustworthy. You know how to build self-esteem and how not to diminish it as well.

You give students a variety of options to choose from in completing assignments and stay after school if a student needs some one-on-one time. You've tried all the new methods you learned in that continuing education course you took over the summer, but nothing has worked.

What else might explain his behavior?

Read on.

Chapter 12

Learning Disabilities

—Tiffany, Age 7—

Tiffany's mother was distraught. "I brought my daughter to you because the teacher says she's not ready for second grade and recommends that she be left back. My husband and I are extremely upset. She's really smart and we don't know what's wrong. Do you think another year in first grade will help her?"

After testing Tiffany, I was able to reassure her parents that she was quite bright, but has dyslexia, a reading disorder. I recommended that she be allowed to go on to second grade and be given additional support in reading.

Sadly, many students like Tiffany are retained because they have an undiagnosed chronic disability that will *not* be cured by repeating a grade. If retained, the child will be another year older with the same impediment to learning and carry the emotional baggage of having been kept back.

This situation is *not* to be confused with retention for a *developmental delay*, which can be of some value. Developmental delays are not learning disabilities. Where the diagnoses of developmental delays are general in nature and suggest that the brain and nervous system will, in time, "catch up," learning disabilities relate to dysfunctions in specific areas of the brain that may permanently affect a child's ability to perform specific tasks and acquire certain skills. These disabilities, each involving different areas of the brain, occur in reading, math and written expression as well as in language processing and attention.

These dysfunctions are not a death sentence to learning material that involves the parts of the brain where the dysfunction occurs. Our brains are amazing organs, especially capable in early life of establishing alternative neural pathways between the sections that must communicate effectively for learning to take place. Finding that you have a learning-disabled child in your class is not unlike coming upon a washed-out bridge on your way to a destination. You don't abandon the trip—you search for a detour. It will likely take longer to get there and more effort, but you can still reach the destination.

Children are generally first diagnosed with learning disabilities when their scores on individually-administered standardized tests fall significantly below norms for other students of the same chronological age, grade level and general intelligence. It has been estimated that between five and 15 percent of students have a learning disability of one type or another.

Some disabilities go undetected, especially if they are mild. Some children are so quiet and cooperative by nature that their issues go unnoticed. Some work hard or use their superior intellects to "get around" their disabilities on their own in the early grades, only to hit a wall in later grades when the material becomes so complex that those compensatory skills no longer help. Others, in defense of their self-esteem, act out inappropriately and are labeled as discipline problems. In these cases, it is neither yours to diagnose nor remediate alone. Call your school psychologist and recommend testing. That's what they're there for.

Fortunately, however, for most students with learning disabilities, the problems are noticed and addressed. If you are concerned that a child in your class may be struggling due to a possible learning disability, you should contact his parents. Speak with the school psychologist and determine what steps must be taken within the policy guidelines of your district in order to have the child evaluated.

The good news is that, once a child's problems are accurately diagnosed, there are many research-based strategies and a wide variety of resources readily available for helping him overcome them.

On the following pages, we've presented a sampling of the most common learning disabilities and have provided brief descriptions of the problems, common symptoms and appropriate remedial teaching strategies.

Reading Disorder - Dyslexia

— Connor, Age 8 —

"What is wrong with Connor?" wondered a teaching assistant. "He just read that word four times on this page and he still doesn't know it!"

Connor had dyslexia — that's why he needed help with reading. But something else was wrong. The teaching assistant in his class was not adequately informed of the symptoms of dyslexia, nor of strategies and techniques for working effectively with a child with this disorder.

Understanding how children learn is critical for teaching *all* children, but especially those with special needs. School is often a stressful environment for these children so if they are not taught with patience and positive reinforcement, they may be "sentenced for life" to poor self-esteem.

Reading is one of the most important skills a child needs to master because it provides a foundation for learning every other subject in school and beyond. Developing reading skills is difficult, especially for those with dyslexia. However, with appropriate intervention, those with dyslexia *can* and *do* learn to read.

Symptoms of a Reading Disorder:

- Has difficulty matching letters and sounds.
- Inserts or deletes words when reading.
- Demonstrates a persistently weak vocabulary.
- Has trouble comprehending what has been read.
- Reads a word but cannot remember it seconds later.
- Cries or becomes upset when asked to read.

Strategies for Working with Dyslexic Students:

- Be sure a thorough diagnosis is made so appropriate remediation tactics can be used.
- A child diagnosed as dyslexic should be taught by a teacher trained in the Orton-Gillingham system. He will need to work on decoding and fluency by learning the phonemes and developing strategies to recall and apply them.
- To make reading easier and to facilitate fluency, have the child memorize commonly used "sight" words.
- Provide easy-to-read books for the child (one or two levels below grade level).
- Have the child read the same books, poems, or plays over and over again. Familiarity improves fluency, as well as retention and confidence.
- Be sure to give the child adequate time. Those with reading problems tend to need more time than average readers because they must use different neural paths when decoding words.
- Play memory games using new sight words and vocabulary words.
- To develop reading for pleasure, have the child select books that are of interest to him. (Recommend books that are on or slightly above grade level to build skills.) Have him read the book aloud with an adult. The child selects a sentence or paragraph on each page that he would like to read. The adult reads the rest of the page.
- Whenever possible, work with the child or have a reading specialist or an assistant do so. Have them read aloud with the child, perhaps alternating paragraphs.

- Use technology to help her read what is needed for her subjects. There are many resources to choose from.
- Have the child follow along in a book that says the words.

Note: If the child reads accurately and fluently and comprehension is the *only* difficulty, then dyslexia is not the issue.

Writing Disorder — Dysgraphia

— Alex, Age 11 —

"How many times am I going to have to tell Alex to begin every sentence with a capital letter?" asked a frustrated teacher in a conference with me.

Alex was a sixth grader who was failing every subject. His parents had exhibited the typical reaction — lecturing that he'd be flipping hamburgers for a career if he didn't get his act together. How, they wondered, could this smart little son of theirs be failing *everything*?

The answer turned out to be a simple one — Alex had a writing disorder, also known as *dysgraphia*. Children with dysgraphia have difficulty with anything involving writing. Their handwriting is poor and they often have trouble with grammar, punctuation, capitalization and spelling, which, in turn, affects their ability to construct sentences and organize paragraphs. Even their math suffers as there is a lot of writing required to do math.

As you might imagine, these children develop a *fear* of writing on top of the neurological dysfunction itself because in school, they are often required to write, rewrite and rewrite again. This takes time for any child, but for those who have a writing disorder, it's torture.

How was Alex failing every subject? Well, he was failing in social studies because the tests were based on notes *copied* from the board and since he wrote so poorly, his notes looked like a chicken had walked across the page. Nobody—not even Alex—could read them. In addition, because he was consumed with the *physical* act of trying to write his notes legibly, he couldn't sustain attention to what the teacher was saying.

He was also failing English because, not knowing what Alex was facing, his teacher required her students to write their reports in cursive script rather than using a computer. Marked down for poor penmanship, his grades on papers were also downgraded for spelling, grammar and punctuation errors.

In math, because of his dysgraphia, Alex couldn't keep numbers lined up—performing accurate calculations was nearly impossible for him, even if he understood the concepts.

And then there was science, where a large part of his grade was based on written lab reports. Unable to write without significant difficulty, he simply gave up.

Because of the frequency with which handwriting is involved in every academic subject, children with dysgraphia face tremendous challenges. It is especially important for these children to be provided with acceptable alternatives for recording notes and assignments and for demonstrating what they've learned, which, after all, is the point.

Symptoms of a Writing Disorder:

- Handwriting is poor.
- Pencil grip is poor or incorrect.
- Artwork is poor relative to that of most of their peers.
- Letters and numbers are often reversed or inverted.
- Can tell you the answers verbally but has difficulty getting those same thoughts onto paper.
- Has difficulty copying from the board.
- Has difficulty copying from a book.
- Avoids assignments requiring writing, whether it be writing words or writing numbers while doing math.
- Complains that his hand hurts when he writes.
- Ends up in tears while doing writing assignments.
- Sits for hours trying to write a paper and accomplishes very little.
- Cannot keep the numbers lined up in columns while doing math computations.
- Has difficulty with spelling and grammar and, therefore, avoids assignments requiring writing.

Strategies for Working with Writing-Disordered Students:

- Encourage your student to use a computer when possible (unless penmanship is the goal of the assignment). If the student hasn't learned to use a computer, introduce him to keyboarding and basic word processing functions. This will give him access to useful spelling and grammar functions, freeing him from some of the mechanical parts of writing. (There are special keyboards available to accommodate those who are 3-8 years of age. See if your school or the PTA would consider providing a few for classroom use.)

- Have your student practice writing individual letters, words, sentences, or short paragraphs at an agreeable time and in manageably brief intervals. Keep the sessions appropriate in length depending on the child's age, maturity level and personality.
- Praise and encourage your student when he writes well to reinforce positive (or simply neutral) feelings toward writing.
- If your student reverses letters, write the correct letters for him so that he can refer to them when necessary. Also, show him the finger trick for b and d using the word bed. Note: *writing* in reverse is *not* dyslexia.
- During a writing session, if your student has trouble spelling, spell the words for her. If the primary goal is writing, focus on writing. Stopping to look up words is tedious and interferes with the creative process. Encourage her to ignore spelling until a draft is written and go back to correct spelling errors after the paper is complete.
- Demonstrate the use the "spell check" feature of most word processing software. (The AutoCorrect function can also be turned on to show spelling mistakes while typing. If this is distracting, the feature can be disabled during composition and a "spell check" run after the project is fully written.)
- Play writing games. For example, give your student one or more words and ask him to write a sentence using them. For each sentence of six or more words completed, give him a small reward.
- Have the student tell you what he wants to write about and you or an assistant can write his thoughts on paper. This can be in list form (sentence fragments

are fine), on a web (main idea in the middle of a circle and thoughts on spokes coming out of the circle) or in outline form. Number the ideas and cross out the ones that do not belong. Decide together which ideas should be written in the beginning, middle and end of the paper. Then have your student write or type out each idea in sequence until the paper is completed.

- Provide adequate time to write. Many kids actually enjoy writing, but may need extra time to organize their thoughts and write them down.
- Avoid requiring excessive rewrites. Forcing a child to rewrite is drudgery that turns him off to writing and contributes to little or no improvement.
- If writing takes an excessively long time, find ways to speed up the process. If necessary, ask parents or aides to write the rough draft as the student dictates and then have the student do the final draft.
- Make arrangements for lengthy writing assignments to be dictated to a parent or adult or into a voice recognition computer program such as Nuance's "Dragon NaturallySpeaking®."
- Use a word bank (a list of key words related to each assignment) that students can readily refer to for correct spelling.
- Consider noting or separately evaluating, but not counting off for spelling. Evaluate maturity of content over technical issues.

Math Disorder — Dyscalculia

—Alexa, Age 12—

"You failed your math test again," said the teacher to Alexa. "Look what you did! You added when it said to subtract. You have to be more careful."

Alexa was a seventh grader who had failed in math every year beginning in first grade. Anything relating to numbers eluded her.

Math is a frustrating subject for many children—either they can't remember number facts or they memorize them in a flash but don't understand or process the associated concepts. Some children experience difficulty with both computation and application, a condition known as dyscalculia. These children have difficulty understanding, recognizing, or naming mathematical symbols, copying numbers or figures correctly, or remembering mathematical steps and sequences.

Symptoms of a Math Disorder:

- Avoids math work of all kinds.
- Becomes confused when encountering math concepts.
- Has trouble with word problems.
- Becomes tearful when required to do math in class or for homework.
- Changes the order of numerals when copying them.
- Cannot keep numbers in columns.
- Adds one column of numbers then switches to subtraction for the next.

- Has difficulty remembering addition and multiplication facts.
- Has difficulty remembering math steps. For example, cannot remember how to carry or borrow numbers, how to do long division, or how to add, subtract, multiply, or divide fractions.

Strategies for Working with Math-Disordered Students:

- If your student has trouble keeping numbers in their columns, have her use the vertical columns on graph paper or lined paper turned sideways.
- Have your student cover up all columns except those she is working on.
- If a child is being tested on math concepts and has difficulty with computation, allow the use of a calculator.
- Suggest that your student circle the "+" or "-" sign before computing the problem.
- Color-code "fact families" and multiplication facts for younger students. For example you color the facts "2+3=5, 3+2=5, 5-2=3, 5-3=2" in green and "3+4=7, 4+3=7, 7-3=4, 7-4=3" in blue.
- Large numbers can intimidate some students, making it difficult to understand a problem. So, when doing word problems, show how to temporarily replace large numbers with easy ones in order to figure out how to "set up" the problem. For example, have students change the numbers in this word problem: "How far will an object traveling 134,000 miles per hour go in 24 hours?" Using 50 miles per hour and two hours instead makes it easier for the student to grasp the need to use multiplication in solving the

problem. Once that's understood, the student can go back and finish the task using the original numbers.

- When working on a word problem, show your student how to organize the "clues" contained in the problem, including what she is being asked to solve. The clues can be organized in any way that works for a given student, e.g., underlining, listing, or making diagrams.
- When appropriate, suggest that your student draw a picture that illustrates the math problem.
- Have your student subvocalize while doing math work.

Expressive or Receptive Language Disorder

—Kathy, Age 14—

Kathy was a tall, slender ninth-grader with whom I had worked since fourth grade. The strategy that had worked best for her was to preview the following week's schoolwork so that she would be more comfortable with the vocabulary and concepts when introduced in class.

One afternoon, Kathy told me that she was having a test on India the next day. I asked her a simple question. "What continent is India on?"

"North America," she replied quickly.

I asked Kathy why she thought India was in North America, and she proceeded to pull out an article the teacher had given the class. The article was about how the cow population had become so large it created a problem in a section of New Delhi called Okla.

Kathy had highlighted the entire article in a variety of pinks, blues, yellows, greens and oranges, but it was clear she had no idea what it was about. She had heard everything the teacher had said in class about the article, but interpreted it to mean that there were cows in Oklahoma (Okla) and they had something to do with a delicatessen (Delhi) and American Indians (India). To set her on the right track, I reached for the globe and used it as we re-read the article together.

When I called Kathy's teacher the next day to discuss my concerns, he was shocked — he had had the map in front of the class throughout the lesson and couldn't understand how Kathy had misinterpreted the information.

Kathy's learning disability, known broadly as "Expressive or Receptive Language Disorder," is characterized by difficulties with output or with processing the inputs of language or both. Some children with this disorder have perfectly good hearing, yet cannot accurately comprehend what has been said to them.

Some are good listeners and others are not. But when it comes to school, those who *are* good listeners have an advantage over those who are not. When a teacher *tells* students everything they need to know for the upcoming test, the students who are good listeners tend to do okay without a lot of effort. (If the student has above average auditory memory, this can be a major advantage for him too.)

On the other hand, students who have poor listening skills may miss most of what is said in class and have to visually *read* the material. Unfortunately, because reading often takes a long time, many kids avoid taking sufficient time to read an assignment thoroughly so as to understand what they read.

—Michael, Age 12—

Another student of ours — a seventh grader named Michael — was struggling in science. When Michael came to me, he told me that his teacher wasn't using a textbook, which meant he had to take notes.

He told me he thought they were learning about somebody named Adam, but he really didn't understand it. After going through his notes carefully, I realized that Michael was learning about atoms, *not Adam. Similar to Kathy, Michael had a receptive language issue.*

Symptoms of an Expressive/Receptive Language Disorder:

- Frequently has trouble understanding oral directions.
- Has trouble remembering exactly what someone says.
- Has trouble taking decipherable notes by hand or otherwise.
- When asked to repeat what has just been said, responds with "I don't know," and means it, because she really *doesn't* know. These children hear the words but *can't put them together in a meaningful and logical way.* In other words, they see the trees but they don't see the forest. When they attempt to find meaning, it's often totally wrong.

Strategies for Working with Students with Expressive or Receptive Language Disorder:

- Show your student how to preview what is happening the next week in school so that she'll be more familiar and comfortable with the vocabulary and the concepts going in.

- When talking with him, without interrogating, ask him to tell you what he thinks you said. If he has no idea or responds incorrectly, explain the information differently.
- Provide visual cues when possible. Instead of just verbally giving a homework assignment, write the assignment on the board. This helps visual learners also.
- Tell your students that it is okay if they don't understand something. Welcome their honesty and try to explain it another way.

ADD/ADHD

—Charlie, Age 14—

"I think I have ADD. I've told my parents that I need medication. My friend takes medicine and he's doing better in school. But my parents won't take me to a doctor. They say that I don't have ADD, that I just have to study.

I've tried to study, but I can't. I can't stay focused. See? I keep fidgeting. Will you tell my parents that I should take medicine for ADD?"

Charlie was a ninth grader who believed his bad grades were due to an attention deficit disorder. When I evaluated Charlie, I saw no indication of ADD. Instead, what I saw was a teenager who had no idea how to study, wasn't interested in school and was a bit immature. He had self-diagnosed and decided that the only way he would succeed was with medication.

I told Charlie that everybody has issues with attention when they're not interested in what is happening and that he needed to change his thoughts.

Having an attentional issue does *not* necessarily mean that a child or adult has ADD or even ADHD (ADHD is an attention deficit problem with physical hyperactivity). In fact, most people have trouble staying focused on what they are doing if the phone rings, if people are talking nearby, if traffic is rushing past the window, or if loud music is playing. Distractions are everywhere, creating an ongoing impediment to focusing even for people with no neurological dysfunction.

In other words, having difficulty sustaining focus is one of the most common problems kids have in class. This is normal. Difficulty focusing is only one of the symptoms seen in children with ADD or ADHD. Other symptoms include difficulty listening, remembering things, staying still, or waiting their turn. According to the *DSM-IV**, the "bible" of psychologists and psychiatrists,

> "Attention-Deficit/Hyperactivity Disorder is a persistent pattern of inattention or hyperactivity-impulsivity that is more frequently displayed and is more severe than is typically observed in individuals at a comparable level of development."

As mentioned, there are many reasons children may demonstrate what seem to be problems with attention. But don't ignore them. If a child's symptoms become excessive and you suspect ADD/ADHD, contact the parents and discuss your observations with your school's psychologist.

---

* Diagnostic and Statistical Manual of Mental Disorders, 4th Edition. American Psychiatric Association, 2000.

Symptoms of ADD/ADHD:

- Has difficulty paying close attention to details or makes careless mistakes on homework or tests.
- Has difficulty sustaining attention at tasks or play.
- Does not seem to listen when spoken to directly.
- Does not follow through with instructions and often fails to finish schoolwork.
- Has persistent difficulty organizing tasks.
- Avoids schoolwork that has to be done over a long period of time, like a term paper or major project.
- Often loses or misplaces books or assignments.
- Becomes distracted easily.
- Seems to "fidget" all the time.
- Has difficulty remaining seated.
- Seems to always want *what* he wants *when* he wants it.

Strategies for Working with Students with ADD/ADHD:

- Try to change activities with reasonable frequency.
- If a student complains that he can't stay focused when reading, suggest he subvocalize. His brain will "hear" the words. This tactic will help him learn the material and will also help him stay focused.
- Speak to the child's parents and recommend that homework and studying be done in intervals no longer than 20 to 30 minutes at a time. Some children can stay better focused if they know a break is coming. The break itself should be about 10 minutes long and should be spent doing something enjoyable, like having a snack, shooting a few baskets or taking a short walk outdoors.

- Remind your student that when he is doing 20-30 minutes of work, he needs to stay on task. This means concentrating, thinking, reading and writing. Have the younger child who needs to practice focusing work in smaller spurts. Allow "play breaks" in between.
- Recommend using a timer when doing homework or studying. This helps to keep on task and work at a good pace. If using a timer distracts or creates anxiety, suggest using a clock to determine when to take breaks.
- Recommend that the student spread out the work over time whenever possible. Studying or writing a report a little each day, rather than in one sitting, makes the process more manageable.
- Suggest that before starting homework or reading a book, your student should think about what he will be learning from the assignment. Doing this will actually increase his focus.
- Demonstrate how to skim books and chapters. Let your student read the title of the chapter and try to guess what that chapter is about. He can see if it follows class notes. Also, suggest he read the headings and look at the pictures and the captions beneath them. When skimming is done, see if he can answer the questions at the end of the chapter before even reading it.
- While reading a textbook or notes in class, have your student stop and ask himself what he just read. Let him write down everything he can remember. If he can't remember much, have him reread the material and write down ideas or draw pictures, graphs, or charts during the process — anything that will help him to stay focused long enough to remember the information.

Open Letter From a Learning-Disabled Teacher

"I have dyslexia. That doesn't make me stupid!"
—Maria, Age 25—

This is an excerpt from an open letter from a student I taught to read years ago. As a student, Maria was not alone. There are countless Marias, Toms and Marks who struggle with dyslexia or other learning disabilities. Due to their disabilities, these students are frequently misunderstood and suffer unnecessary blows to self-esteem. Often unusually perceptive and creative, they are seldom treated with the respect they deserve.

> *"I've had dyslexia all my life. That made learning to read very difficult for me," Maria told me. "When I was in school, I was so frustrated with anything involving reading that I wanted to scream. In fact, my dyslexia made school a living hell.*
>
> *"Teachers would give me work and say, 'Do the best you can.' Duh, I couldn't even read the directions on the top of the sheet, so I just sat there not knowing what to do. All they kept saying was, 'Maria, do your work!'*
>
> *"One day when I was trying to read a sentence, one of the kids said out loud, 'That's the same word you just read. What are you, stupid?' And, you guessed it – the whole class heard it and laughed at me. I ran out of the room so they wouldn't see me crying.*
>
> *"It was a long hard road, but I learned how to compensate – to overcome my dyslexia – so now I am able to read just about as well as normal readers. What took me even longer to learn is that I am all right – that I am not stupid. In fact, I finished college and earned a masters de-*

gree in special education. I am now a special-ed teacher and I enjoy helping students who have learning disabilities.

"Thanks to brain research, the dyslexia 'dark ages' are rapidly coming to a close. Teachers and other reading specialists now know that dyslexia is not "reading backwards"; it is a learning disability due to a dysfunction centered in the language portion of the brain. With appropriate intervention, dyslexia can be overcome.

"I am also writing this secretly wishing it were possible to deliver the message to all kids who have dyslexia or any other type of learning disability. They need to know that they are not alone, that they can believe in themselves and even more importantly, that they are not stupid."

Teachers and other school personnel are generally wonderful, hard-working people who care about their profession and the children they are charged with educating. But sometimes we don't take the time to learn about a child's limitations or how to adapt lesson plans to allow them to develop the alternative strategies they will need to circumvent obstacles in their paths.

Before concluding that a student is lazy, stupid, or defiant, look for symptoms of a learning disability. Contact his parents and share your observations with school personnel. If you know a child has problems and see that another teacher may be unaware of his issues, share this book or any information regarding the disorder with them.

As Maria said and knows all too well, kids with learning disabilities need to know they are not alone, that their difficulty has no relationship to their importance to you, that it is possible for them can overcome obstacles and succeed academically, and that you will help them do just that.

Like anyone, they need to believe in themselves and have confidence that they have the skills to handle whatever obstacles they encounter. And the first step to developing that confidence is to know you believe in them, too.

Chapter 13

Other Obstacles to Learning

—James, Age 13—

*"I don't want to do homework. I hate school," said
James.*

"He's just lazy," said his father.

I turned to James. "Are you good on your skateboard?"

*"Yeah," replied James quickly. "I can do jumps and
all kinds of tricks."*

*I turned back to Dad. "Based on that, I know he's not
lazy. He's simply not motivated to do schoolwork."*

By no means are learning disabilities the only obstacles
that stand in the way of learning. Throughout life, everyone
encounters obstacles that prevent us from succeeding.

The following represent the most common obstacles
we've seen that stand in the way of academic achievement.
I like to call the first three obstacles "The Three 'Tions'"
(pronounced "shuns") and the rest "The Terrible 'Toos.'"

The Three "Tions"

Obstacle 1: Lack of Motivation

Lack of motivation is one of the biggest obstacles teachers must help students overcome to help them do well in school. Research has shown that motivation comes from within. As a result, when students are truly unmotivated, it's very difficult to push them. The old adage is true—you can lead a horse to water but you can't make him drink.

Let's face it. Nobody's motivated to feel badly about themselves. James, in the opening example, obviously felt proud of the skills he'd developed while riding his skateboard, hence his eagerness to engage. He was motivated to talk about and demonstrate his prowess there.

It's safe to say, then, that for unmotivated students, the connection between school achievement and self-esteem has not been well-established.

So what can you, as a teacher, do to influence motivation? Find out what interests them, what gives them trouble, where their talents and challenges lie and then focus on providing an environment where they can experience true academic success. Be sure to involve parents whenever possible.

Also, reward them in an age-appropriate way. Everyone loves recognition. To younger kids use the usual smiley-faces and gold stars. With older ones, have an awards ceremony and give out certificates to those who work hard, get high grades, create outstanding projects, improve the most, or meet other individual academic benchmarks. Develop an achievement "point system" where students get points they can exchange.

To have genuine achievement recognized and acknowledged by their teachers not only motivates students to achieve, but also promotes self-esteem.

Obstacle 2: Disorganization

—Randy, Age 13—

The first time Randy came to our office with his mother, I noticed that he was carrying a book bag the size of a small refrigerator. He sat silently while his mom talked continuously about his disorganization. Randy seemed detached, as if the conversation had nothing to do with him. It was as if he had just come along for the ride.

When I asked Randy why he thought he was there, he replied that he had no idea. He seemed genuinely perplexed — it was obvious that he didn't think he had a problem. Mom took the lead and asked him if we could peek inside his book bag.

"It's OK with me," said Randy, as a big smile formed on his face. "But I'm warning you — opening this bag can be hazardous to your health!"

We all laughed, but Randy was right. As we opened the top flap of his overloaded bag, papers, books, notebooks, chewing gum wrappers, paper airplanes, old notices, overdue assignments and gym clothes tumbled out.

"Randy," I said, "you don't think there's a problem?"

"It's not my problem," he answered. "The teachers don't let you go to your locker except during lunch. And I'm afraid I'll forget things — no, I'm sure I'll forget things — and my teachers will go crazy. So, I cover all my bases and keep everything in my book bag."

Indeed, Randy *was* covering all his bases. He carried the contents of his entire locker around with him all day! In an attempt to deal with his organization problem, he had developed a strategy that he believed worked for him. It did, but only in the sense that he never lost anything, evidenced by his pet phrase: "Hang in there, I'll find it—it's in here somewhere." While Randy found a solution to keeping his papers and possessions in one place, he hadn't discovered a way to keep everything organized.

We went to work. I gave Randy a red, three-ring, loose-leaf notebook with dividers. Together, we plowed through his book bag, sorted the loose pages and after punching holes in them, placed them in their correct sections: math, English, history, science, Spanish. Some papers we tossed into the paper-recycling bin.

We also created a section for time management sheets and other items that he'd eventually need. Then, I gave Randy a new assignment book and we proceeded to put together a plan of attack. After an hour of working on organization, Randy was beaming—he was proud of himself. I saw Randy for a few more sessions. Not only did his grades go up, but he also felt great.

This kind of organization may seem simple but it is missing from the lives of many children. We often see children who are overwhelmed by the amount of schoolwork and homework they have to do and have difficulty organizing their papers and assignments. As a result, they lose track of what's due when and often give up altogether.

Encourage kids to allow enough time for each assignment. Most of what we do takes longer than anticipated and, for many students, the agenda is more about how *quickly* homework can be done so they can move on to fun stuff. Being organized can help make homework preparation more efficient so that students can complete their assignments and still have time to pursue outside hobbies and activities.

Establishing priorities

Even those students who understand the value of short-term goals don't always have the skills to prioritize them. They may need help evaluating which activities are more important, which assignment should be done first, which can be skipped, if need be. You can help by explaining the importance of doing homework either before or after playing (depending on an individual child's physiological needs) or by suggesting which subject to do first. For example, if a student finds math easy but her handwriting deteriorates as she gets tired, you might suggest that she do her English homework first.

Organizing Paperwork

As I did with Randy, recommend that your students gather all the notes, handouts and papers that they collect and, throughout the year, keep them all in one place — in one notebook, one folder, or one section of a folder with multiple pockets. Show them that when it's time to prepare for a test, they can easily go to the appropriate location and find what they need to study. (It may motivate them to be organized if you tip them off that tests and quizzes will many times come directly from those notes and handouts.)

Suggest that students organize their papers first by subject (English, math, history, etc.) and then organize those papers by topic. They can even go a step further by organizing each topic by subtopic, if they choose.

Organizing Time

Time management skills are beneficial for all students —
and teachers, too. When students use time wisely, they can
study more efficiently and, in turn, get maximum grades in
the least amount of time.

Strategies Teachers Can Use to Help
the Disorganized Student

- Be a good role model. If your students see that you're
  organized, they will have someone to emulate. (If you
  have difficulty with organization, buy some books
  or go on line to find strategies dealing with how to
  get organized yourself! Remember, follow your own
  rules...)
- Buy a quality three-hole punch for your class and
  recommend that each student buy an inexpensive one
  to keep in his backpack.
- Be sure your students have and use an assignment
  book or other aid. Encourage your students to use
  colored book covers — one color for each subject — or
  have them use clear wrap or clear book covers, so that
  they can always see which book is which.
- Suggest that students separate morning books from
  afternoon books, e.g., keep books needed for morning
  classes on the top shelf of their lockers and afternoon
  books on the bottom.
- Help your students devise lists and schedules that
  work for them.

For visual learners especially, having and using a time management grid or a similar paper or electronic calendar, allows students to see, at a glance, what assignments, projects and tests are upcoming in any given week or month. With our students, we use grids like that shown on the next page. Directions for how to use the grid follow. Feel free to create your own and distribute to interested students.

Directions for the Time Management Grid

Use light colored pencils or a highlighter. Write the name of the activity in the boxes before coloring.

Use one color to color-in boxes related to **school** items:

1. Box in the hours at school.
2. Box in the hours spent in after-school activities.
3. Box in the hours working after-school (for high schoolers).
4. Box in the hours needed to get ready for school, have dinner and sleep.

Use a second color for **non-school** activities:

5. Box in the TV shows that are "must" watch.
6. Box in the time spent on the telephone or other medium meeting with or talking to friends.
7. Box in the time spent going out with friends or family.
8. Box in the activities done on the weekends. Use a third color to color in boxes related to homework
9. Box in the time needed to study and do homework.

TIME MANAGEMENT GRID							
Time	Mon	Tue	Wed	Thu	Fri	Sat	Sun
6:00							
7:00							
8:00							
9:00							
10:00							
11:00							
12:00							
1:00							
2:00							
3:00							
4:00							
5:00							
6:00							
7:00							
8:00							
9:00							
10:00							
11:00							

Obstacle 3: Procrastination

> *"Did you do your homework?" asked Mom.*
>
> *"No problem, Mom," Luke replied. "I'm going to do my homework, but first, I need to get a snack."*
>
> *Later: "Luke, did you start your homework?"*
>
> *"I'm gonna start just as soon as this show's over. Trust me, Mom."*
>
> *Much Later: "Luke, did you do your homework?"*
>
> *"No problem, Mom. Just have to call someone about something."*

Luke intends to do his homework. He's motivated to get good grades. He may even be organized. And though he truly *believes* that he's going to do it, somehow, his homework rarely gets done. Luke suffers from the third "Tion," Procrastination.

Get procrastinators moving by starting their homework in school. If they need to write an essay, help them with the first few sentences. If they have difficulty getting started with math or science problems, do the first few with them. Often, once these kids get started, they will continue because they're on a roll. Sometimes they just need a nudge.

The "Terrible Toos"

Obstacle 4: Working Too Slowly

Even without learning disabilities, some students work too slowly, so they need more time than others to do almost anything. This includes writing down assignments, completing assignments and taking tests. These students seem to be driven by a slower clock. They even tie their shoes slowly. These students are perpetually playing "Beat the Clock," which is surely anxiety producing.

Strategies and Recommendations for Students
Who Work Too Slowly

- Try to set aside extra time so these slower moving students will be able to complete the tasks they need to function in your class. This includes copying notes, writing down assignments, doing class work and taking tests. If after allocating more time, they're still unable to finish, encourage them to discuss the matter with you. There may be an undetected issue that needs attention.
- Look for timesaving options. Consider shortening assignments (for example, assigning all the even numbers or odd numbers on the math page instead of the entire page) or permitting those who need it time to finish some assignments over the weekend. Also, for these students, try to keep classroom distractions to a minimum.

- Get approval for extended time. If a student is classified with a learning disability and he works particularly slowly, be sure that extended time for tests and modification for homework is part of his I.E.P. (Individual Educational Plan).
- Remember that learning is not a race. If a child is not classified as learning disabled and is struggling because of time, see what you can do first to alleviate the situation. The main goal of school is to educate, however and if a child cannot learn because of the speed at which school is moving, talk to the school counselor, social worker, psychologist or principal to see if there's another way to provide the extra time he needs.

Obstacle 5: Too Tired to Study

As discussed in the chapter on needs, when we don't get enough sleep, the brain and body do not work well. When a student doesn't get enough sleep, she feels tired, has trouble concentrating and has trouble controlling her temper. A lack of sleep affects everything about us: our personalities, our ability to comprehend and remember information and our ability to focus.

Strategies and Recommendations

- Review the student's schedule. If homework is being pushed until late at night, work with your student and her parents to try to adjust her schedule.
- Have the school nurse talk to your class or PTA about the need for adequate amount of sleep.

Obstacle 6: Too Stressed

Everyone has personal problems at one time or another. These problems tend to cause stress. Sometimes even minor problems are blown out of proportion and appear to be more important than they are causing an inordinate amount of stress.

Stress is not the exclusive domain of adults. Children and teens also have personal problems that cause stress. Students might have had an argument with a parent, a friend or another teacher. They might have lost a grandparent. They may be caught in the middle of an ugly divorce. The list goes on and on. The teen years are especially stressful. Hormones are raging and peer pressure is at an all time high. School, college admissions and thinking about the future, are often center stage when it comes to stress. Some kids worry so much about grades and testing, SAT or ACT scores, or college admissions that it's hard for them to think about anything else.

The overstressed child has trouble concentrating, relaxing, studying properly, sleeping and succeeding in school. Research has shown that stress actually changes the brain to the point that prevents us from thinking sharply or properly.

If you suspect that a student suffers excessively from stress, contact her parents or the school psychologist.

Strategies and Recommendations:

- Think about whether you may be inadvertently causing the stress. As a teacher, are you speaking or acting in a way that might create tension, fear, or pressure? Are your standards so high that students feel stressed trying to meet them? If so, consider making some changes in your behavior, expectations, or the manner in which you are teaching.

- Are any of your students at the breaking point? If you think so, contact the parents and school psychologist. Everyone's potential for stress is different; everyone's personality is unique. What may be easy for one child in your class to deal with may not be so easy for another.

Obstacle 7: Too Much Multitasking

It's not that kids aren't trying to study—most are. And it's not that they don't care—most do. But we are now living in a time and culture unlike any before. E-mailing, texting, phoning, playing video games—it's multitasking on steroids.

What we've known for a long time has been confirmed by recent research: performance *suffers* when people do more than one thing at a time. In fact, when people go from one task to another very quickly, they are actually slowed down.

Assess, Don't Assume

At one time or another in their academic lives, all students will face obstacles that are too hard for them to manage alone. Sometimes those obstacles come in the form of learning disabilities, sometimes in other forms.

As teachers, we will always be our students' best allies in conquering challenges at school. But a crucial first step to conquering any obstacle is accurate assessment of what the obstacle is. The very same behaviors can be symptoms of very different problems—so the key is remembering that accurate diagnosis relies on observation of a *pattern* of symptoms, not a single symptom itself.

Embarking on a remedial plan to help your students overcome obstacles that don't exist is to create yet another obstacle. If you think you see evidence of one of the many things we've talked about, record your observations and share them with your student's parents, guidance counselor or school psychologist.

Chapter 14

12 Strategies for Improving Memory and Recall

"Did you study?" asked the teacher.
"Yes," said the student.
"Then how could you fail this test? It came right from your notes!"

I'm always amused when, after a kid fails a test, a teacher or parent asks him, "Did you study?" Of course, the answer is always yes. So why does he fail? As we've discussed, there are many possible explanations, but sometimes the answer is actually quite simple—*he doesn't know how to study*. And productive studying depends on the developed ability to *remember* what one has learned in class. It's all about memory.

Learning depends on storage of information in long-term memory. As we discussed earlier, when information doesn't remain in short-term memory for at least 30 seconds, it often doesn't make it into long-term storage. Learning requires *memorization* and *repetition*—as demonstrated by actors learning their lines or baseball players in the batting cage.

Students who regularly seem to succeed have usually developed their own strategies for retaining material—ones they pick up over the years. But others, particularly those in elementary or middle school, haven't yet developed these skills and sometimes don't even know how to begin. If that stands in the way of learning, it is our responsibility to help them develop those skills. Here are the top 12 strategies we use in our tutoring practice for enhancing that process:

- Understanding
- Chunking
- Visualizing
- Associating
- Rhyming
- Talking
- Storytelling
- Memory Sentences
- Acronyms
- Reviewing
- Graphic Organizers
- Playing Games

Strategy 1: Understanding

Precious time and energy is wasted when teachers don't check to make sure their students understand the concepts and vocabulary they use when presenting new material. It's easy to forget that students, especially young ones, don't necessarily have the same common reference points or the range of experiences that adults do. Children are often not familiar with the words teachers use or the references they make. You can't teach the principles of magnetism to someone who has never seen a magnet.

If a student doesn't have a handle on the general

concepts on which you're basing a lesson, he'll be lost when it comes to knowing what information to memorize. Here are general ideas for facilitating your students' better understanding.

- When introducing a new unit, connect new information to things your students are likely to have experienced or learned, including important material from the previous lesson. It's much easier for us to understand new things when they are connected to ideas already stored in memory.
- Take a multisensory approach to teaching any subject and you'll have a greater chance of reaching the majority of students. Use a variety of verbal, written, visual and other sensory-based methods to convey the same basic information.
- Demonstrate and use concrete examples whenever possible. For example, if you're teaching geography, have a globe or map available so students can visualize the area in a global context. When teaching the concept of balancing equations, bring out a double-panned balance.

Strategy 2: Chunking

Once students understand new material, divide it into smaller segments so they can more easily memorize it. This is called "chunking."

We use chunking to remember information in our everyday lives—telephone numbers, postal codes and Social Security numbers are grouped into small chunks.

The reason is that it's easier for us to remember three, four or five bits of information at a time. That's the key to chunking—memorizing a small group of items before moving on to another one. The "right" number of items depends on the individual and the subject.

- To help your students memorize vocabulary words, chunk them by parts of speech or another suitable category—put all the nouns together, etc. If there is no obvious pattern, put the words together in groups of no more than five at a time.
- Chunk history topics according to time periods or events. For example, the Revolutionary War can be divided into three chunks: what led to the war, the war itself and the results of the war. List for your students the pivotal events in each group or chunk. (The "Boston Tea Party," for example, would be placed under the "what led to the war" category.)
- Have students memorize material for literature by listing events or scenes in each chapter.
- Use chunking with learning a foreign language by grouping the words by categories. For example, group words for household items, school items, or occupations together.
- If you or your students use flash cards with success, chunk those by category as well.

Strategy 3: Visualizing

To visualize means to "see" an image in your mind without actually looking at the material object. For students who have trouble visualizing, it is helpful to use maps, charts, graphs (bar, line, pie, pictograph, etc.) or pictures to accompany the lesson. If you encourage students to draw their own pictures, they will first need to visualize the material in order to draw a picture. By default, the practice of drawing a visual image will help them remember more of what they are learning.

Strategy 4: Associating

Have your students associate words with a person, place, thing, feeling, or situation. Suggest that they connect words, especially adjectives, with someone they know, e.g., "Altruistic" Alice or "Lethargic" Larry. (Alliteration helps association, too.)

One little girl we knew confused the Atlantic and Pacific Oceans, until her Uncle Pete from California taught her how to swim in the Pacific Ocean. She never got them mixed up again, because she remembered, "Pete swims in the Pacific."

Strategy 5: Rhyming

Rhyming is another strategy that has helped millions remember and store information. As noted before, most of us learned the alphabet by reciting (or even singing) the "Alphabet Song." There's also the vowel-trick rhyme: "'i' before 'e' except after 'c.'" And as we all know, "30 days has September, April, June and November…"

Encourage students to create rhymes about pivotal facts or events they are learning in history, science, literature and even some math calculation rules. Get the whole class involved in creating the rhymes — this way, they'll be more inclined to use them. Here are some examples of rhymes used for learning multiplication facts:

- 7 and 7 went down the line to capture number 49.
- 8 and 4 made some stew and gave it to 32.
- 8 and 8 went to the store to buy Nintendo 64.

The last one is dated, but works surprisingly well. The sentence doesn't have to make sense — the rhyme's the thing.

Strategy 6: Talking

Here's a strategy that's easy and fun to use, especially for students who like to talk! Have them tell others about what they are learning — including their parents, siblings, friends, or grandparents. (If people aren't available, talking to pets or stuffed animals works well, too.) If a topic lends itself to different viewpoints, a friendly debate encourages students to create new connections.

Simply repeating something aloud helps us hold it in short-term memory so it can be stored in long-term memory. For example:

- **History.** Talking about history helps get facts into long-term memory. Have your students pretend they lived during the era or in the countries they're studying. Have them select a famous person who was part of a major historical event and, pretending to be that character, talk from their point of view about pivotal events. They can talk about what happened, where it happened, who was involved and the outcome. This type of role-play allows students to learn history from the inside, because they are not just talking about it, but, in their imagination, they're experiencing it.

- **Foreign Languages.** When learning a foreign language, encourage students to speak it with others at school during lunch or recess or at home at the dinner table. It makes no difference whether others know what they are saying — it can even be more fun if they don't — but speaking the language out loud reinforces what has been learned and how to use it.

- **English Vocabulary Words.** The best way to learn new vocabulary words is to use them! Assign exercises that have students intentionally using the new words they're learning when talking with friends or family members. The more they use the words, the more the words will become part of their ever-growing vocabularies.

Strategy 7: Storytelling

Storytelling is a great way for students to use and remember information on any subject — it fosters creativity and facilitates getting information into long-term memory. Students "refresh" their memories every time they tell a story. Unlike talking, which is simply engaging someone else (or even talking to yourself) about a subject, storytelling requires focusing on key points and demands that we arrange them in a logical sequence.

And there's a bonus. Each event in a logical story triggers memory of the next event. When telling a story, your students will often remember details they thought they'd forgotten! For double effect, encourage them to use *pictures* to tell stories as another way to enhance the experience and the memorization process. They may even want to draw cartoons or put together a little book about the material they're learning.

Strategy 8: Creating Memory Sentences

Creating sentences using the first letters of important facts to remember builds on Strategy 4. Students can create memory sentences for virtually any subject. For example, when learning the order of operations in math, students find it easier to remember the sentence, "Please excuse my dear Aunt Sally." The first letter in each word of the sentence equates to a single math component, as shown:

Please = Parentheses	**Excuse = Exponents**	**My = Multiplication**
Dear = Division	**Aunt = Addition**	**Sally = Subtraction**

Here's another sentence that many students have used to remember the planets of the solar system: **My Very Excellent Mom Just Served Us Nine Pizzas.**

The first letter of each word in the sentence corresponds with the name and order of their distance from the sun of the nine planets: Mercury, Venus, Earth, Mars, Jupiter, Saturn, Uranus, Neptune and Pluto. (Of course, since Pluto was recently demoted, we need to modify the memory sentence to something like, "**My Very Excellent Mom Just Served Us Noodles,**" but you get the point.)

Strategy 9: Using Acronyms

Similar in form to a memory sentence, acronyms are words created from the first letters of a list of words. (Technically, if the acronym is a nonsense word, it's called an "initialism.") Here's how it works: Students take a list of words or facts that they want to remember and put them in an order so that the first letters (or syllables) of each word spell another word. For example, to memorize the names of the five Great Lakes, students often remember the word "HOMES": H=Huron, O=Ontario, M=Michigan, E=Erie and S=Superior.

Here are some examples of acronyms that started out as initialisms, but have been assimilated into our language as words:

- NASA = National Aeronautics and Space Administration
- SCUBA = self-contained underwater breathing apparatus
- RADAR = radio detection and ranging
- LASER = light amplification by stimulated emission of radiation

Strategy 10: Reviewing & Practicing

As mentioned before, when we first learn something, it's stored in short-term memory. But short-term memory only holds information for up to a minute. That's not much help for a test that's three weeks away. In order to remember material for the test, this information needs to be stored in *long-term* memory.

How does it get there? As we said in the beginning of this chapter, *reviewing* and *practicing* material facilitates its being encoded into long-term memory so it'll be there later when needed.

Practice reinforces and enhances the effectiveness of most strategies relating to learning. For instance, students can "practice" subjects like social studies and science by re-reading notes that have been chunked into smaller pieces. They can practice subjects like math by doing assigned homework problems. They can learn foreign languages by repeatedly speaking words aloud and prepare for music recitals by playing pieces over and over. Repetition is key.

Helpful Hints for Reviewing and Practicing

- When working on their own, suggest that students review and practice for short time periods (perhaps 20 to 30 minutes) and then take a ten-minute break to call a friend, have a snack, shoot some hoops, etc.
- Have them use a multisensory approach every time they review or practice a subject by talking aloud, writing, reading, drawing, singing, or doing something physical. They'll figure out which works best for them.
- Many students find that reviewing or practicing lessons before bedtime is a good way to study and get material into long term memory. Bedtime, of course, should be at a reasonable hour—a good night's sleep helps with retention, too.
- Suggest they review or practice in the morning, if possible, while brushing teeth, eating breakfast or riding to school.

Strategy 11: Using Graphic Organizers

Building on Strategy 3, Visualization, use formalized visual representations of tasks to explain and review concepts in class. Remind students to go over them again when doing homework and studying for tests as well.

Below and on the next page are examples of graphic organizers we use to help frame abstract concepts.

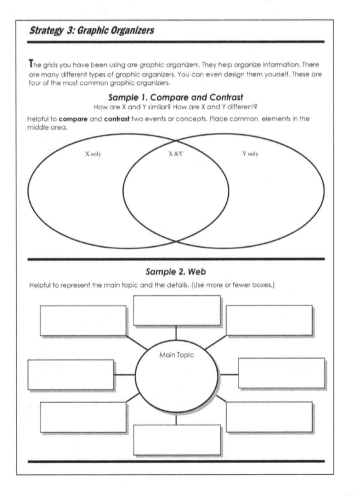

Strategy 3: Graphic Organizers

The grids you have been using are *graphic organizers*. They help organize information. There are many different types of graphic organizers. You can even design them yourself. These are four of the most common graphic organizers.

Sample 1. Compare and Contrast
How are X and Y similar? How are X and Y different?

Helpful to **compare** and **contrast** two events or concepts. Place common elements in the middle area.

X only   X & Y   Y only

Sample 2. Web
Helpful to represent the main topic and the details. (Use more or fewer boxes.)

Main Topic

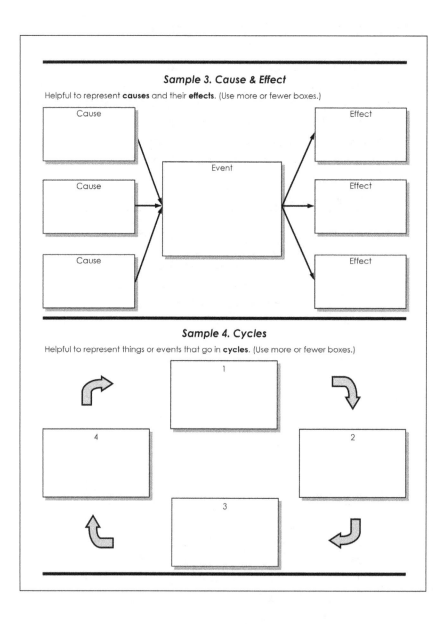

Sample 3. Cause & Effect

Helpful to represent **causes** and their **effects**. (Use more or fewer boxes.)

Cause

Cause

Cause

Event

Effect

Effect

Effect

Sample 4. Cycles

Helpful to represent things or events that go in **cycles**. (Use more or fewer boxes.)

1

2

3

4

Strategy 12: Playing Games

Playing games can be a great way to learn new material, especially if they're fun and engaging and provide unlimited opportunity for purposeful repetition.

Here are some games that you can introduce and play with students at any grade level. In some cases, a student can play alone as well as with others.

The Match Game

Subjects: All
Players: 1 or more
Equipment: Index cards (cut in half if you wish)

1. Make a "question" deck of cards by writing one chunk of information to be learned on one side of each card. This can be a word, phrase, formula, anything.
2. Number each card on the back.
3. Make one answer card for each question card using different color card or ink. These become part of the "answer" deck. Write the matching number on the back of each card.
4. Shuffle the cards, keeping the two decks separate.

Rules (For one player):
1. Arrange all of the "question" cards face up on a table.
2. Turn over one "answer" card at a time and try to find the matching question.
3. Check the backs to confirm the match and place the matches on a "match" pile.
4. Game is won when all cards are in the "match" pile.

Rules (For two or more players):

1. Arrange all of the "question" cards face up on a table.
2. Place the "answer" deck on the table, answer side down.
3. The first player picks the top "answer" card and tries to find the matching question on the first try.
4. If the cards match, the player puts both cards in his "match" pile. If the cards do not match, the player places the answer card on the bottom of the "answer" deck.
5. Play continues in a clockwise direction as each player takes one turn.
6. The game ends when all the question cards are matched. The winner is the player with the most matches.

Twenty Questions

Subjects: All
Players: 2 or more
Equipment: None

Rules:

1. Player 1 thinks of something all players have to know.
2. The other players take turns asking up to 20 questions to try to guess what Player 1 is thinking.
3. Player 1 can only answer "yes" or "no."
4. The object is to make a correct guess using as few questions as possible.

Fact Stack

Subjects: All
Players: 2 or more
Equipment: None

Rules:
1. Player 1 states one bit of information about a topic that all players are trying to learn.
2. Player 2 repeats the first bit of information and adds another bit of information to the "stack."
3. The play continues as each player repeats all of the information in order and adds one more bit of information to the "stack."
4. The first player to make a mistake is out.
5. The last player remaining is the winner.

You Got It

Subjects: All
Players: 1 or more
Equipment: Index cards (cut in half if you wish)

1. Make a deck of cards by writing one chunk of information to be learned on one side of each card. This can be a word, phrase, formula, or anything.
2. Write the companion answer-word or phrase in another color on the other side of each card.
3. Turn all the cards answer side down and shuffle the deck.

Rules (For one player):

1. Pick up one card at a time. If you know the information on the card, put it into your "you got it" pile. If you do not, put it on the bottom of the deck.
2. You win when all cards are in your "you got it" pile.

Rules (For two or more players):

1. The dealer deals one card to each player answer side down.
2. Starting with the player to the dealer's left, each person tries to answer or explain the information on the card. Each player who does so correctly puts the card on his "you got it" pile.
3. Remaining cards are returned to the bottom of the deck.
4. The dealer deals another card to each player answer side down.
5. The play continues until there aren't enough cards to deal.

The winner is the one with the most "you got it" cards.

Chapter 15

Students and Homework

The purpose of homework is:

A. To give students opportunity to review what they learned in class.
B. To give students opportunity to *pre*view what they will be discussed in class.
C. So teachers can prove they've covered all concepts mandated by the Common Core curriculum.
D. To facilitate student learning.
E. All of the above.

Because there is more information kids need to know and more skills they need to master to be able to compete in this information-driven global economy, the amount of homework seems to have increased in the past few years. As the amount has increased, the effectiveness of homework as a way of reinforcing material discussed in class has decreased. More and more kids rush through piles of homework—not necessarily learning anything from it, not always completing it and not always handing it in.

In order to meet demands from administrators, teachers are pressured to cover the specifics of an ever-expanding curriculum, which seems to increase the need for homework, but the very same time constraints often make it impossible for most to even check if the homework is done correctly, much less go over the answers in class.

For younger children, homework often curtails or displaces time to play, denying them valuable experiences that, like recess, help grow their bodies and minds.

This chapter offers suggested guidelines for how teachers may begin to solve the homework conundrum. These guidelines can be easily adapted for use in an individual classroom or as the basis for discussion with those tasked with establishing school- or district-wide homework policy.

But, as with everything else we as educators say and do, the singular question we must ask and answer is:

Does it help students learn?

Sixteen Guidelines for Homework Assignments

1. Ensure that homework is purposeful.

If children, particularly older ones, perceive that homework is purposeful, they're far more likely to buy into it and do it well. In our view, there are three main purposes of homework, which give rise to the "**Three-Step Homework Plan" or "RAP"**:

R = Review what was done in class in order to ensure comprehension.
A = Apply and practice exercises relating to the material covered during class.
P = Preview the material that will be covered in class the next day.

Reviewing and applying what was done in class has been the main purpose of homework forever. With the advent of the Common Core State Standards, using homework time to *preview* is now coming into its own. It's a brilliant way to help make learning easier and more efficient. Previewing is like a "sneak peek" — it allows students to see what will be covered the next day in class to help them get more out of the lesson.

2. Ensure that the quality of your homework assignments is consistent with that of your classroom instruction.

Students are quick to notice and react to "low-quality" homework, which we define as not fulfilling an obvious purpose. Examine the homework assignments you've given in the past and consider finding ways to "upgrade" any of them, if necessary. Here are a few suggestions:

- If the textbook homework questions are poor quality or don't relate to what you taught in class, don't use them. Assign only those items that reinforce classroom exposure.
- Supplement textbook items with quality homework questions or tasks that you borrow from other sources or create yourself.
- When selecting items to include in your homework assignments, be sure to include some that require both lower and higher-order thinking skills.

Assembling great homework items requires an investment of time, but it is time well spent — once done, you'll likely be able to use the assignments or simply add to them for many years to come.

3. Remember that homework "quantity" does not correlate to homework "quality."

Many teachers assign a considerable amount of homework, believing it demonstrates that they've covered the material required by the curriculum.

But, homework isn't about quantity. *Homework is about helping children learn.* Limit the number of items assigned to correspond with the realistically-assessed capacity of your students.

For example, let's say the homework suggested in a textbook consists of 50 exercises. Avoid assigning all 50. Students will concentrate while doing the first one, a little less while doing the second one and will likely do the remaining 48 on auto-pilot. They won't be thinking at all, but simply pushing a pencil around.

John, an algebra teacher, told me that when he assigns homework, he makes a deal with his students. If they promise to do all the homework he assigns — to really try on each problem, concentrating on using the strategies he showed them in class *for the entire time allotted* — then he'll assign only 10 or 15 equations. If not, they have to complete 50 equations in one sitting. He reports that his students see this as a "good deal." They "buy into" the arrangement and tend to do the homework.

But he doesn't stop there. John allocates class time the following day to provide answers and to go over difficult or problematic questions so his students learn how to do them correctly. If he sees that his students need more practice, he will assign another 10 or 15 of the same type of item for homework and repeat the process until he's sure virtually all of his students understand. And that, after all, is the point of homework, isn't it?

4. Be an ally with homework, not an adversary.

You'll be amazed how kids will learn to trust you once they perceive that you really *are* on their team. If you're fair, assign homework that's reasonable and valuable and care enough about them to review their work and provide the support they need, it will dramatically reduce the homework challenges you face. For older students, once you establish a trusting relationship, you can save valuable class time by simply providing your students with the answers and letting them come to you only if they have problems. (Those few who are inclined to cheat will do it anyway — the rest will be able to check that they're doing the work correctly and will be able to get much more out of their homework sessions.)

5. Use the ten-minute rule.

There is no set rule as to how much homework is the right amount, but remember to consider the age of your students and their not-yet-full-grown capacities for attention and understanding. The ten-minute rule has proven reasonable in the past: Multiply the grade level by 10 minutes and that's approximately the right amount of time children should have to spend doing all their homework each night. For example, grade 1 – 10 minutes, grade 4 – 40 minutes, grade 12 – 120 minutes. This will vary considerably, depending on subjects, projects due, upcoming tests, etc. and may be slightly longer on weekends, as needed, to complete major projects or prepare for exams. If your students consistently take more time doing their homework night after night, give thought to modifying your assignments. (Also see *Collaborate with Colleagues* below.)

6. Encourage your students to use assignment books or an electronic equivalent.

Assignment books are tools that help students keep on top of the assignments and project deadlines. Many students have assignment sheets that can be hole-punched and put at the front of their binders; others log assignment in separate notebooks or notepads. There are even those who download and use phone apps that allow them to record assignments. Regardless of the method your students prefer, make sure they know how to use them effectively.

On the facing page is a sheet we've been giving to students in our Strong Learning Centers for many years. (Feel free to use this for your classes.)

_**Month:**_____**Day:**_____**Year:**_____

Cut when all assignments are done ✂

✓ Things to take home:	Textbook	Workbook	Papers	Assignments	Due Date	Test Date
English/ Language Arts ☐ ✓ HW Done						
Reading ☐ ✓ HW Done						
Math ☐ ✓ HW Done						
Social Studies ☐ ✓ HW Done						
Science ☐ ✓ HW Done						
☐ ✓ HW Done						
☐ ✓ HW Done						

Other things to take home:	Things to bring to school:
1._____	1._____
2._____	2._____
3._____	3._____
Message for Parents:	Message for Teachers:

Remind your students to cut the upper right hand corner only after all assignments are completed. Thus, if there is a long term assignment, the corner tab will remain un-cut as a reminder.

7. Recommend or provide assignment calendars and grids.

Have students write long-term assignments on a large calendar. This helps to manage the workload.

8. Write homework assignments on the board.

Be sure to give homework assignments visually as well as orally to accommodate learning styles and disabilities. Online redundancy, now commonly set up on school or district wide websites, is also useful. Be consistent. Always write the assignment in the same way and in the same place. Provide enough time for students to copy the instructions in their assignment books or onto their electronic devices. Since some students need the extra help writing their assignments, you may need to double check that everyone has recorded the homework assignment properly.

9. If it's algebra homework, don't grade on English.

Homework grades, if any, should be based on the assignment, and only on the assignment itself. If the purpose is to learn how to construct a geometric proof, avoid the temptation to take off points because of spelling or grammar errors. Note the errors if you like, but leave the grading of grammar to English teachers.

10. If you assign it, go over it.

—Sally, Age 12—

"I have to know this for a test tomorrow," said Sally. She handed me homework from the day before. It consisted of 50 questions. The teacher had placed a big red checkmark and a smiley face at the top. I noticed, however, that more than half the questions had been answered incorrectly.

"Sally," I said, "Most of these are wrong. Didn't the teacher go over the answers during class?"

"No," she answered. "We never do, so it doesn't matter if they're wrong."

We've mentioned this before, but it's important enough to mention it again. If you assign homework, go over it in class or provide answers so the students can check their answers. Otherwise, doing the homework is a waste of their time and they know it.

This is particularly problematic when it comes to summer packets. In recent years, many schools have begun to require kids to do massive packets over the summer to be handed in for credit the first day of school. There are many good reasons for kids to remain academically active during the summer. However, if kids learn from experience that their work won't be checked and no feedback given, they'll have little motivation to take the work seriously.

11. Avoid requiring too much "stuff."

Disorganized students can't get out of their own way as it is. They need all the help they can get, so be kind. Don't overwhelm them by requiring multiple notebooks.

For most students, one loose-leaf notebook with dividers is much easier to deal with. Similarly, don't overload them with a gazillion handouts. Too many duplicated pages invite disaster.

The same can be said for projects. Long-term projects are great but make sure they're not too complex. Some teachers assign projects that are so complicated that they would take an executive and a full staff a month to complete. Try to be realistic about your students' capabilities and their already overly-full schedules.

12. Collaborate with colleagues about homework assignments.

Middle and high school teachers often need to talk among themselves to keep informed about what's being assigned in other subjects. If left to chance alone, there'll be many times when there's a homework bubble—that is, an unusually large amount of homework or tests that fall on the same day.

This creates an untenable situation for kids that serves no useful purpose for anyone. By making your colleagues aware of when you plan to schedule major projects, an occasional massive homework assignment, or major tests, they may be able to adjust what they assign to balance the load on your mutual students. Work together.

13. Offer homework rewards.

Especially for younger students, offer little rewards at the end of each day, or week, if they complete all their homework assignments. The reward can be anything—a smiley-face stamped on their page or a sticker. A little reward can be just the motivation your students need to help them stay on task.

Use group pressure occasionally, giving the whole class a special prize or special consideration (for example, extra time at recess or no homework on Friday) if everyone hands in their homework that week.

14. Remember that children need breaks.

Encourage your students to take short breaks during long homework sessions. Recommend that they walk around, shoot a few baskets, or get a snack. Their brains will work more efficiently with the increased blood flow.

15. Help students organize their books.

- Color-code textbooks to ensure that the right one(s) are taken home. (Colored book covers or labels can be used — a different color for each subject.)
- Alternatively, suggest the use of clear book covers or clear plastic to cover the books, so that students can always see the covers.
- If all else fails, you can suggest that parents request an extra set of books to keep at home. If the school cannot provide them, ask the parent to order them. Next year's parents will be happy to take them off their hands.

16. Keep records for motivation.

Help your students learn how to keep a record of their grades. The purpose of keeping a record is to help establish goals and monitor progress. Assure them that these records are solely for them—and their parents—to see progress and create goals for improvement. Again, let your students know that you're on their side and care about their academic achievement. Teach them to monitor their own progress, take responsibility for getting their homework done and above all, take credit for their successes.

When Kids Fail to Do Homework

If a student fails to do homework, look into *why* instead of automatically giving zeroes or punishing a student. Check with the guidance counselor and the student's parents. Be flexible and understanding. There's almost always a reason and it's usually something you can help rectify.

- **Make it easy to make up homework when reasons for missing it are valid.** When a student misses a homework assignment because he's sick, there are issues at home, or even if he goes away for a family vacation, work out with the student and his family how and when the assignment will be completed. While your assignment is important to you and it will help the child learn, there may be times when other issues take priority in that child's life. Take time to uncover reasons or stumbling blocks and then find ways for the child to cover the material and make up the assignment.
- **Communicate with parents.** If a student continually neglects his homework, notify the parents that you are concerned. Arrange for a brief conference with the parent(s) to discuss the problem. If the parents seem angry about their child's negligence, when appropriate, recommend that they consider what

possible contributing factors may be at play. If the opportunity presents itself, remind them that calling their child "lazy" and punishing him not only won't help solve the problem, but will most likely create more problems.

- **If missed homework assignments are habitual, look for an unrelated, underlying cause.** Perhaps a student feels that his peers won't accept him if he does his work. One bright, good-looking middle school student with raging hormones stopped doing schoolwork and homework because he was terrified that the "ladies" in his class would find out that he was smart and he wouldn't appear to be "cool."

- **Consider that some students simply don't want to do the homework.** Remember, too, that the resistance may not always be simply stubbornness. Though some kids just won't do it because it isn't fun, some kids write down and do their assignments only to have their parents require them to do the work again and again to meet unreasonable standards — which is precisely what the student is trying to avoid. Not doing the homework solves that problem for them, at the cost of creating others. The option is theirs to choose.

Because many children and teens live for the present, they don't always connect their actions with consequences. If this is the case, talk to the child about logical consequences, e.g., failing, having to attend summer school, or being retained. Interestingly, even if a child does "get" the connection, punishing him for not doing homework doesn't always work, because many students see punishment is a lesser evil. In fact, some children even *seek* retention over doing homework because it's easier for them to handle.

The goal of homework is to familiarize students with information and concepts that have been or will be discussed in class and reinforce mastery of the concepts following the class discussion. If the homework you assign doesn't result in learning, it's your responsibility to find out why.

Conclusion

It is our sincere hope that in these pages, we provided you with a renewed understanding of the mission of education and practical suggestions for how to create and maintain environments where kids learn while meeting the demands of *our* workplace at the same time.

As we said in the beginning, we believe that bad grades happen to good teachers when they lose focus on our mission and are distracted by things we can't control.

The knowledge and skills required in our world and the tools available to students expand every day, but our students' basic human needs haven't changed. And it has long been supported by research that if these needs are not met in our classrooms, our ability to do our jobs is diminished, if not compromised completely.

As those adults to whom students look for guidance second only to their parents, it falls to us not only to impart the skills and subject matter knowledge they need to thrive in the workplace, but to facilitate their ability to learn it by giving them experience in setting goals, in making sound decisions, in managing the obstacles they will no doubt encounter and in developing the self-esteem and confidence they will need to succeed both in our classrooms and long after they've gone.

It is also our responsibility to remember that *we are learners as well as teachers* and always have room to grow and improve. Achieving our primary goal—to provide environments where learning has the greatest chance to occur—requires that we, too, commit to a process of continuous improvement in our own skills and knowledge.

The good news is that all students want to succeed in school and, with guidance, can make the grade.

And if *they* make the grade, so will we.

Appendix

The Common Core Standards
The InTASC Standards
The Danielson Framework &
The **STRONG** Learning Model

The Common Core State Standards were released in 2010 for implementation in 2014. The InTASC standards for professional educators were released in 2011. Together, they provide measurable baselines for the two-part mission of educators—to provide students with the knowledge and skills they will need to grow and thrive as individuals and valued contributors in the workplace and to society in general (CCSS) and a system for evaluating the proficiency of new and veteran teachers in creating an environment in which students have the greatest opportunity to learn (InTASC).

The criteria used by a committee of leaders in government, business, and education to develop the Common Core State Standards were that they be:

- *Aligned with college and work expectations;*
- *Include rigorous content and application of knowledge through high-order skills;*
- *Built upon strengths and lessons of current state standards;*
- *Informed by top-performing countries, so that all students are prepared to succeed in our global economy and society; and,*
- *Evidence and/or research-based."** *

The summary document detailing the InTASC standards reads,

*"The updating of the core teaching standards was driven not only by new understandings of learners and learning but also by the new imperative that every student can and must achieve to high standards. Educators are now being held to new levels of accountability for improved student outcomes. These standards embrace this new emphasis and describe what effective teaching that leads to improved student achievement looks like. They are based on our best understanding of current research on teaching practice with the acknowledgment that how students learn and strategies for engaging learners are evolving more quickly than ever ..."** *

---

*Introduction to the Common Core State Standards, June 2, 2010

**InTASC Model Core Teaching Standards: A Resource for State Dialogue, April 2011, p. 3

For your reference, on the following pages we have reprinted:

- The InTASC Standards with expanded explanations as excerpted from a PDF downloadable on the CCSSO website (*www.ccsso.org);*
- A summary of the domains of the Danielson Framework for teacher evaluation, including the 22 components comprising those domains;
- Charts reproduced from the Danielson site (*www. danielsongroup.org*) showing the alignment of the Danielson Framework with the InTASC standards;
- A chart detailing how each of the sub-domains of the Danielson Framework relate to the ideas and principles of the STRONG Model, and
- One more reminder that the mission of education is to help children LEARN.

Interstate Teacher Assessment and Support Consortium (InTASC)

The InTASC standards as excerpted from the InTASC website at:

http://www.ccsso.org/Documents/2011/InTASC_Model_Core_Teaching_Standards_2011.pdf, pp. 8-9

The Learner and Learning

Teaching begins with the learner. To ensure that each student learns new knowledge and skills, teachers must understand that learning and developmental patterns vary among individuals, that learners bring unique individual differences to the learning process, and that learners need supportive and safe learning environments to thrive. Effective teachers have high expectations for each and every learner and implement developmentally appropriate, challenging learning experiences within a variety of learning environments that help all learners meet high standards and reach their full potential. Teachers do this by combining a base of professional knowledge, including an understanding of how cognitive, linguistic, social, emotional, and physical development occurs, with the recognition that learners are individuals who bring differing personal and family backgrounds, skills, abilities, perspectives, talents and interests. Teachers collaborate with learners, colleagues, school leaders, families, members of the learners' communities, and community organizations to better understand their students and maximize their learning. Teachers promote learners' acceptance of responsibility for their own learning and collaborate with them to ensure the effective design and implementation of both self-directed and collaborative learning.

- **Standard #1: Learner Development.** The teacher understands how learners grow and develop, recognizing that patterns of learning and development vary individually within and across the cognitive, linguistic, social, emotional, and physical areas, and designs and implements developmentally appropriate and challenging learning experiences.

- **Standard #2: Learning Differences.** The teacher uses understanding of individual differences and diverse cultures and communities to ensure inclusive learning environments that enable each learner to meet high standards.

- **Standard #3: Learning Environments.** The teacher works with others to create environments that support individual and collaborative learning, and that encourage positive social interaction, active engagement in learning, and self-motivation.

Content

Teachers must have a deep and flexible understanding of their content areas and be able to draw upon content knowledge as they work with learners to access information, apply knowledge in real world settings, and address meaningful issues to assure learner mastery of the content.

Today's teachers make content knowledge accessible to learners by using multiple means of communication, including digital media and information technology. They integrate cross-disciplinary skills (e.g., critical thinking, problem solving, creativity, communication) to help learners use content to propose solutions, forge new understandings, solve problems, and imagine possibilities. Finally, teachers make content knowledge relevant to learners by connecting it to local, state, national, and global issues.

- **Standard #4: Content Knowledge.** The teacher understands the central concepts, tools of inquiry, and structures of the discipline(s) he or she teaches and creates learning experiences that make the discipline accessible and meaningful for learners to assure mastery of the content.

- **Standard #5: Application of Content.** The teacher understands how to connect concepts and use differing perspectives to engage learners in critical thinking, creativity, and collaborative problem solving related to authentic local and global issues.

Instructional Practice

Effective instructional practice requires that teachers understand and integrate assessment, planning, and instructional strategies in coordinated and engaging ways. Beginning with their end or goal, teachers first identify student learning objectives and content standards and align assessments to those objectives. Teachers understand how to design, implement and interpret results from a range of formative and summative assessments. This knowledge is integrated into instructional practice so that teachers have access to information that can be used to provide immediate feedback to reinforce student learning and to modify instruction. Planning focuses on using a variety of appropriate and targeted instructional strategies to address diverse ways of learning, to incorporate new technologies to maximize and individualize learning, and to allow learners to take charge of their own learning and do it in creative ways.

- **Standard #6: Assessment.** The teacher understands and uses multiple methods of assessment to engage learners in their own growth, to monitor learner progress, and to guide the teacher's and learner's decision making.

- **Standard #7: Planning for Instruction.** The teacher plans instruction that supports every student in meeting rigorous learning goals by drawing upon knowledge of content areas, curriculum, cross-disciplinary skills, and pedagogy, as well as knowledge of learners and the community context.

- **Standard #8: Instructional Strategies.** The teacher understands and uses a variety of instructional strategies to encourage learners to develop deep understanding of content areas and their connections, and to build skills to apply knowledge in meaningful ways.

Professional Responsibility

Creating and supporting safe, productive learning environments that result in learners achieving at the highest levels is a teacher's primary responsibility. To do this well, teachers must engage in meaningful and intensive professional learning and self-renewal by regularly examining practice through ongoing study, self-reflection, and collaboration. A cycle of continuous self-improvement is enhanced by leadership, collegial support, and collaboration. Active engagement in professional learning and collaboration results in the discovery and implementation of better practice for the purpose of improved teaching and learning. Teachers also contribute to improving instructional practices that meet learners' needs and accomplish their school's mission and goals. Teachers benefit from and participate in collaboration with learners, families, colleagues, other school professionals, and community members. Teachers demonstrate leadership by modeling ethical behavior, contributing to positive changes in practice, and advancing their profession.

- **Standard #9: Professional Learning and Ethical Practice.** The teacher engages in ongoing professional learning and uses evidence to continually evaluate his/her practice, particularly the effects of his/her choices and actions on others (learners, families, other professionals, and the community), and adapts practice to meet the needs of each learner.

- **Standard #10: Leadership and Collaboration.** The teacher seeks appropriate leadership roles and opportunities to take responsibility for student learning, to collaborate with learners, families, colleagues, other school professionals, and community members to ensure learner growth, and to advance the profession.

The Danielson Framework for Teacher Evaluation
www.danielsongroup.org

Domain 1—Planning and Preparation

1a: Demonstrating Knowledge of Content and Pedagogy
1b: Demonstrating Knowledge of Students
1c: Setting Instructional Outcomes
1d: Demonstrating Knowledge of Resources
1e: Designing Coherent Instruction
1f: Designing Student Assessments

Domain 2—Classroom Environment

2a: Creating an Environment of Respect and Rapport
2b: Establishing a Culture for Learning
2c: Managing Classroom Procedures
2d: Managing Student Behavior
2e: Organizing Physical Space

Domain 3—Instruction

3a: Communicating With Students
3b: Using Questioning and Discussion Techniques
3c: Engaging Students in Learning
3d: Using Assessment in Instruction
3e: Demonstrating Flexibility and Responsiveness

Domain 4—Professional Responsibilities

4a: Reflecting on Teaching
4b: Maintaining Accurate Records
4c: Communicating with Families
4d: Participating in a Professional Community
4e: Growing and Developing Professionally
4f: Showing Professionalism

Correlation between the **Danielson Framework for Teaching** and the **Interstate Teacher Assessment and Support Consortium (InTASC) Standards**

Council of Chief State School Officers – ccsso.org

page 1 of 3

InTASC Standard	Danielson Framework Component(s)
#1. Learner Development The teacher understands how learners grow and develop, recognizing that patterns of learning and development vary individually within and across the cognitive, linguistic, social, emotional, and physical areas, and designs and implements developmentally appropriate and challenging learning experiences.	**Planning and Preparation** 1b: Demonstrating Knowledge of Students 1c: Setting Instructional Outcomes 1e: Designing Coherent instruction **Instruction** 3c: Engaging Students in Learning
#2: Learning Differences. The teacher uses understanding of individual differences and diverse cultures and communities to ensure inclusive learning environments that enable each learner to meet high standards.	**Planning and Preparation** 1b: Demonstrating Knowledge of Students
#3: Learning Environment The teacher works with others to create environments that support individual and collaborative learning, and that encourage positive social interaction, active engagement in learning, and self-motivation.	**Classroom Environment** 2a: Creating an Environment of Respect and Rapport **Instruction** 3c: Engaging Students in Learning
#4: Content Knowledge. The teacher understands the central concepts, tools of inquiry, and structures of the discipline(s) he or she teaches and creates learning experiences that make the discipline accessible and meaningful for learners to assure mastery of the content.	**Planning and Preparation** 1a. Demonstrating Knowledge of Content and Pedagogy 1e: Designing Coherent instruction **Instruction** 3c: Engaging Students in Learning

Correlation between the **Danielson Framework for Teaching** and the
Interstate Teacher Assessment and Support Consortium (InTASC) Standards
Council of Chief State School Officers – ccsso.org

InTASC Standard	Danielson Framework Component(s)
#5: Application of Content. The teacher understands how to connect concepts and use differing perspectives to engage learners in critical thinking, creativity, and collaborative problem solving related to authentic local and global issues.	**Instruction** 3a: Communicating with Students 3c: Engaging Students in Learning 3f: Demonstrating Flexibility and Responsiveness
#6: Assessment. The teacher understands and uses multiple methods of assessment to engage learners in their own growth, to monitor learner progress, and to guide the teacher's and learner's decision making.	**Planning and Preparation** 1f: Designing Student Assessments **Instruction** 3d: Using Assessment in Instruction
#7: Planning for Instruction. The teacher plans instruction that supports every student in meeting rigorous learning goals by drawing upon knowledge of content areas, curriculum, cross-disciplinary skills, and pedagogy, as well as knowledge of learners and the community context.	**Planning and Preparation** 1b: Demonstrating knowledge of students 1e: Designing coherent instruction
#8: Instructional Strategies. The teacher understands and uses a variety of instructional strategies to encourage learners to develop deep understanding of content areas and their connections, and to build skills to apply knowledge in meaningful ways.	**Instruction** 3b: Using Questioning and Discussion Techniques 3c: Engaging students in learning

Correlation of Danielson Framework for Teaching to InTASC Standards

THE DANIELSON GROUP

Correlation between the Danielson Framework for Teaching and the Interstate Teacher Assessment and Support Consortium (InTASC) Standards

Council of Chief State School Officers – ccsso.org

InTASC Standard	Danielson Framework Component(s)
#9: Professional Learning and Ethical Practice. The teacher engages in ongoing professional learning and uses evidence to continually evaluate his/her practice, particularly the effects of his/her choices and actions on others (learners, families, other professionals, and the community), and adapts practice to meet the needs of each learner.	**Professional Responsibilities** 4a: Reflecting on Teaching 4e: Growing and Developing Professionally 4f: Showing Professionalism
#10: Leadership and Collaboration. The teacher seeks appropriate leadership roles and opportunities to take responsibility for student learning, to collaborate with learners, families, colleagues, other school professionals, and community members to ensure learner growth, and to advance the profession.	**Professional Responsibilities** 4c: Communicating with Families 4d: Participating in a Professional Community 4f: Showing Professionalism

Correlation of Danielson Framework for Teaching to InTASC Standards

THE DANIELSON FRAMEWORK

THE STRONG MODEL

THE DANIELSON FRAMEWORK	Self-Esteem	Trust	Responsibility	Options	Needs	Goals
Domain 1: Planning and Preparation						
1a: Demonstrating Knowledge of Content and Pedagogy		X	X			
1b: Demonstrating Knowledge of Students	X	X	X			
1c: Setting Instructional Outcomes			X			X
1d: Demonstrating Knowledge of Resources			X	X		
1e: Designing Coherent Instruction	X	X	X	X		X
1f: Designing Student Assessments	X	X	X	X	X	X
Domain 2: Classroom Environment						
2a: Creating an Environment of Respect and Rapport	X	X	X			X
2b: Establishing a Culture for Learning	X	X	X	X	X	X
2c: Managing Classroom Procedures		X	X			
2d: Managing Student Behavior	X	X	X	X	X	X
2e: Organizing Physical Space			X			
Domain 3: Instruction						
3a: Communicating with Students	X	X	X	X		X
3b: Using Questioning and Discussion Techniques			X	X	X	X
3c: Engaging Students in Learning	X	X	X	X	X	X
3d: Using Assessment in Instruction	X		X	X		X
3e: Demonstrating Flexibility and Responsiveness	X	X	X		X	
Domain 4: Professional Responsibilities						
4a: Reflecting on Teaching	X	X	X	X	X	X
4b: Maintaining Accurate Records		X	X			
4c: Communicating with Families	X	X	X			X
4d: Participating in a Professional Community			X			
4e: Growing and Developing Professionally	X		X			X
4f: Showing Professionalism		X	X			

REMEMBER...
Bad grades don't happen to good teachers when they create environments where all students
LEARN

L	**LEVEL ASSESSMENT** - Assess the current LEVEL of the student. Begin where the student is and build on that.
E	**ENGAGEMENT** - ENGAGE students through all their senses. Teach to all learning styles.
A	**ACTIVATION** - ACTIVATE the body to motivate the mind. Ensure basic needs are met, from hunger to play.
R	**REHEARSAL** - REHEARSE at each leg of the journey. Provide opportunity to practice—from simple recall to extended thinking.
N	**NEURONAL CHANGE** - Change the NEURONS. If it isn't stored in long-term memory, it hasn't been learned.

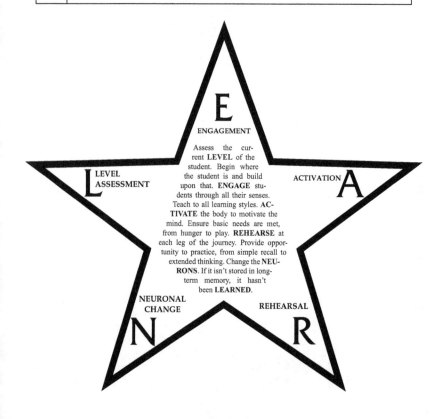

Selected Resources for Teachers

Note: This resource list is not intended as a comprehensive bibliography or a resource list for all the topics covered in Why Bad Grades Happen to Good Teachers. Most books (and other media) in the list emphasize classroom strategies that can be implemented today.

Learning Resources and Services from Strong Learning

http://www.StrongLearningTeacherStore.com

Danielson Demystified:
A Companion Casebook for
Why Bad Grades Happen to Good Teachers

Also find a variety of fun, research-based games, workbooks and ebooks for use in the classroom and as homework assignments

---

ADD/ADHD

Delivered from Distraction. Edward M. Hallowell, M.D. and John J. Ratey, M.D. Ballantine Books, 2005. See chapters 1-3 and 23.

The Gift of ADHD Activity Book: 101 Ways to Turn Your Child's Problems into Strengths. Lara Honos-Web, Ph.D. New Harbinger Publications, 2007. Most activities can easily be modified for the classroom.

All About ADHD: The Complete Practical Guide for Classroom Teachers. Linda Pfiffner. Scholastic Teaching Resources, 2nd Edition, 2011

Classroom Communication

The Compassionate Classroom: Relationship Based Teaching and Learning. Sura Hart and Victoria Kindle Hodson. Center for Non-violent Communication and PuddleDancer Press, 2004

Beyond Discipline: From Compliance to Community. Alfie Kohn. Association for Supervision and Curriculum Development, 10th Anniversary edition, 2006

Cognitive Thinking and Brain-based Learning

Brain-Based Learning: The New Paradigm of Teaching. Eric Jensen. Corwin Press, 2nd ed., 2008

Working Memory and Learning: A Practical Guide for Teachers. Susan Gathercole and Tracy Packiam Alloway. Sage Publications, 2008.

Emotional Resilience

Building Emotional Intelligence: Techniques to Cultivate Inner Strength in Children. Linda Lantieri, with Introduction and Practices by Daniel Goleman, 2008. Sounds True Inc.

The Educator's Guide to Emotional Intelligence and Academic Achievement: Social-Emotional Learning in the Classroom. Maurice Elias and Harriett Arnold, Editors, 2006. Corwin Press

HeartMath tools, training, programs and education applications from the Institute of HeartMath — an effective and research-proven program for building emotional resilience in the classroom. *http://www.heartmath.org/education/education-home/education-applications.html.*

Exercise, Physical Fitness and Movement-based Learning

Spark: The Revolutionary New Science of Exercise and the Brain. John Ratey, M.D. Little, Brown and Company, 2008. See Chapters 1 and 6.

Movement Based Learning for Children of All Abilities. Cecilia Koester, M.Ed., 2006. Focus on children with mental and physical disorders but useful for all children.

Learning Disorders

Overcoming Dyslexia: A New and Complete Science-Based Program for Reading Problems at Any Level. Sally Shaywitz, M.D. Vintage, 2005.

Teaching Kids with Mental Health & Learning Disorders in the Regular Classroom: How to Recognize, Understand and Help Challenged (and Challenging) Students Succeed. Miles L. Cooley. Free Spirit Publishing, 2007.

Learning Styles and Multiple Intelligences

The Unschooled Mind: How Children Think and How Schools Should Teach. Howard Gardner. Basic Books, 2nd ed., 2011

Multiple Intelligences in the Classroom. Thomas Armstrong. Association for Supervision & Curriculum Development, 3rd ed., 2009

Acknowledgments

Thanks to Vally Sharpe for editing, layout, and in general for working so closely with us in the final editing stages.

And to the thousands of clients over the years who placed their trust in us and their academic lives in our hands. *We* trust that many thousands more will be STRONG because of what we learned from *you*.

About the Authors

Linda & Alvin Silbert have dedicated over 40 years to the growth and enhancement of children's intellectual, emotional and social development. They have written over 50 books for children from three to 103, which have sold over one million copies.

The Silberts lecture and lead workshops and have appeared on radio and television throughout the U.S. & Canada. They continue to collaborate as writers, educational therapists and directors of Strong Learning Centers, based in New York.

To learn more about Strong Learning Centers or correspond with the Silberts, please visit:

DrLindasBlog.com

or their website devoted to teachers:

www.StrongLearningTeacherStore.com